I0411872

Bureau of
Medicine and Surgery
Washington, D.C. 20372-5300   NAVMED P-5055(August 2001)

Radiation Health Protection Manual

RECORD OF PAGE CHANGES
RADIATION HEALTH PROTECTION MANUAL

Page change	Date of change	Date entered	Signature

LIST OF EFFECTIVE PAGES

CONTENTS

Chapter 1
INTRODUCTION

1-1. Purpose

(1) This manual provides the radiation health requirements applicable to Navy and Marine Corps radiation protection programs. A radiation protection program may be defined as the sum of all methods, plans, and procedures used to protect the health and environment of personnel from exposure to sources of ionizing radiation. It includes the radiation health program and radiological controls program. A radiation health protection program is not an end in itself; its purpose is to provide the means to preserve and maintain the health of personnel while they accomplish necessary and purposeful work in or around areas contaminated with radioactive material or areas where they are exposed to ionizing radiation.

1-2. Scope

(1) These regulations are intended for observance during peacetime by all Navy and Marine Corps activities possessing or using sources of ionizing radiation which may affect the health of personnel. These standards do not apply to the exposure of an individual to ionizing radiation when used for the diagnosis or treatment of medical or dental conditions of that individual. Personnel not employed by the Department of the Navy shall comply in all respects with these regulations when engaged in a Navy-sponsored program or operation. It is recognized that these regulations may not be applicable to procedures initiated after an attack in which nuclear weapons are used; however, the provisions of these regulations, insofar as they are feasible, shall remain in effect after such an attack.

1-3. Policy

(1) Exposure to personnel from ionizing radiation shall be reduced to levels as low as reasonably achievable (ALARA). Positive efforts shall be made to fulfill this objective without compromising operational and training efforts.

(2) Personnel engaged in work in which they may be exposed to ionizing radiation shall be indoctrinated/trained in radiological controls/radiation safety practices and protective measures.

(3) Supervisors of personnel working with radioactive materials or devices that produce ionizing radiation shall be aware of their responsibilities with regard to the execution of safety and protective measures.

(4) Proper protective equipment, and training in its use, shall be available to and used by all occupationally exposed personnel.

1-4. Responsibilities

(1) *General.* Federal regulations for radiation protection are issued by the Nuclear Regulatory Commission (NRC), Department of Health and Human Services, Department of Labor, Department of Transportation, and the Environmental Protection Agency. Instructions, manuals and work procedures are issued by the Department of Defense, Chief of Naval Operations, fleet commanders in chief, systems commanders, type commanders, and commanding officers.

(2) *Chief of Naval Operations (CNO) and the Commandant of the Marine Corps (CMC).* The CNO and CMC shall exercise overall coordination and policy control of the radiation protection programs under their cognizance in the fields of organization, equipment, safety, personnel qualifications, assignments, and training.

(3) *Deputy Chief of Naval Operations, Fleet Readiness & Logistics (N4).* The Deputy CNO (Fleet Readiness & Logistics) is responsible for:

(a) Maintaining a NRC Specific License of Broad Scope (License) for regulated sources used by the Navy and Marine Corps.

(b) Maintaining a Naval Radiation Safety Committee to issue Radioactive Material Permits to individual commands and activities for the use and possession of NRC regulated sources.

(c) Enforcing compliance with Nuclear Regulatory Commission regulations relative to the use of NRC sources and management of the License.

(4) *Chief, Bureau of Medicine and Surgery (BUMED).* BUMED is responsible for approving and issuing requirements for the radiation health protection program applicable to all Navy and Marine Corps activities and for management of the Medical Department's radiation protection program. BUMED is specifically responsible for:

(a) Developing physical standards for personnel.

(b) Applying established radiation protection standards and guidelines.

(c) Investigating physiological effects of radiation.

(d) Conducting radiation medical examinations and providing treatment of radiation casualties.

(e) Approving personnel dosimetry programs.

(f) Establishing training programs and qualification standards for Medical Department personnel involved in radiation health programs.

(g) Reviewing and approving radiation health programs.

(5) *Commander, Naval Sea Systems Command (NAVSEASYSCOM).* NAVSEASYSCOM is responsible for:

(a) Coordinating Systems Command functions related to the radiological controls programs in the areas of industrial (Radiological Affairs Support Program) and weapons (Nuclear Weapons Radiological Controls Program) applications.

(b) Developing procedures and providing technical support and training in the area of radiation safety as assigned in NAVSEAINST 5100.18 series.

(c) Developing and procuring RADIAC instruments and systems, i.e., any equipment used to detect or measure ionizing radiation and specialized equipment used for test/calibration of radiac equipment. Equipment for nuclear reactor control and instrumentation is not included.

(d) Establishing procedures for possession, use and disposal of radioactive material other than medical isotopes, weapons and naval nuclear reactors and associated equipment.

(e) Managing the Navy Low Level Radioactive Waste Program. (See Chapter 7.)

(6) *Director, Naval Nuclear Propulsion Program.* The Director, Naval Nuclear Propulsion Program, per Presidential Executive Order 12344 of February 1, 1982, is responsible for:

(a) Control of radiation and radioactivity associated with naval nuclear propulsion activities.

(b) Prescribing and enforcing standards and regulations for these areas as they affect the environment and the safety and health of workers, and the general public.

(7) *Commanders.* Commanders having command jurisdiction over installations and activities using radiation sources shall:

(a) Take such action as deemed necessary to establish uniform practices and procedures by subordinate commanders and to assure compliance with and implementation of Federal Regulations, Department of Defense directives, and Department of the Navy directives.

(b) Conduct periodic inspections to assure compliance with the applicable directives.

(c) For installations and activities using sources licensed by the Nuclear Regulatory Commission (NRC) and permitted by the Chief of Naval Operations, ensure compliance with provisions of the command's Radioactive Material Permit and with Title 10, Code of Federal Regulations in the use of these sources.

(8) *Commanding Officers and Officers in Charge.* Commanding officers and officers in charge of Navy or Marine Corps activities where military and civilian personnel may be exposed to ionizing radiation shall:

(a) Maintain a Radiation Health Protection Program. The Radiation Health Protection Program will be administered by the command's medical department and shall be supervised by the radiation health officer or his assigned equivalent.

(b) Comply with Federal Regulations and Department of the Navy directives to ensure safety in the procurement, control, storage, handling, use, and disposal of radiation sources and radioactive material in the command's custody. Ensure coordination between the radiation health and radiological controls aspects of the radiation protection program.

(c) Ensure radiation workers have a radiation medical examination prior to being occupationally exposed to ionizing radiation. If it is known a visitor is to perform duties which require a radiation medical examination, the individual's parent organization shall determine the individual's medical qualification for occupational exposure to ionizing radiation and shall provide the facility with the individual's current radiation exposure information.

(d) Ensure that measures are established for controlling ionizing radiation sources so that the radiation exposure to individuals under his command or within his jurisdiction is as low as reasonably achievable and no greater than the limits prescribed herein.

(1) Provide and maintain an appropriate radiation monitoring capability to verify personnel do not exceed the prescribed exposure limits. Chapter 4 provides these limits. Chapter 6 details environmental, area, and personnel monitoring requirements.

(2) Ensure appropriate protective clothing, respiratory protection, and decontamination facilities, as necessary, are provided for personnel handling unsealed radioactive material.

(3) Ensure areas where radioactive materials are used or stored, radiation areas, high radiation areas, very high radiation areas, airborne radioactivity areas, and contaminated areas are posted per Federal regulations and/or Navy directives.

(e) Ensure that the dosimetry results for radiation workers are provided to the custodian of the individual's medical record or to the individual's civilian employer, recorded and reported following the requirements in Chapter 5.

(f) Ensure the health record custodian documents all personnel monitoring results for occupational exposures to ionizing radiation in the health records and that individual health record entries (DD Form 1141 or NAVMED Form 6470/10) and all supporting records are correct, concise, and in agreement with instructions contained in Chapter 5.

(g) Ensure accurate and timely submissions of situational and annual reports to the Naval Dosimetry Center.

(h) At activities holding Radioactive Material Permits under the Navy's Nuclear Regulatory Commission (NRC) license, ensure that a copy of the Radioactive Material Permit together with its amendments and related correspondence, and such other records as necessary to meet the conditions of the Permit are maintained.

(i) Ensure personnel receive radiation protection training commensurate with their duties and per Federal regulations, Department of the Navy directives, program radiological controls manuals, and this manual.

(9) *Naval Dosimetry Center.* The Officer in Charge of the Naval Dosimetry Center is responsible for:

(a) Providing centralized processing and consultation for thermoluminescent dosimeters (the DT-648 dosimeter, the DT-518 accident dosimeter, and LiF extremity dosimeters) and special purpose dosimeters. The Center shall ensure the above mentioned dosimetry systems meet the appropriate calibration standards and shall maintain equipment, calibration sources, and a staff capable of evaluating the various types of dosimeters.

(b) Providing technical assistance when requested on matters regarding personnel dosimetry.

(c) Maintaining a repository of radiation exposure history information for Navy and Marine Corps personnel that allows retention and retrieval of reported radiation exposure data.

(d) Notifying appropriate authorities of irregularities in the reports or indications of an exposure control problem at an activity.

(e) Preparing summary reports of the exposure of Navy and Marine Corps personnel.

(10) *Individual*. Individuals assigned to duties as radiation workers are responsible for:

(a) Reporting the following to their supervisor or medical department personnel in a timely manner:

(1) Any physical condition which they feel affects their qualification to receive occupational exposure.

(2) Any radiation therapy treatment received.

(3) Any radiopharmaceutical received for diagnosis or treatment.

(4) Any occupational radiation exposure received from secondary or temporary employment.

(5) Any open wounds or lesions.

(b) Wearing a personnel monitoring device at all times in any area where monitoring is required. The individual is responsible for loss of, or damage to such a device while in his possession.

(c) Knowing their current quarter and annual Total Effective Dose Equivalent. This information may be obtained from the health record custodian or radiation health/safety officer.

1-5. Definitions

(1) *Absorbed Dose*. The energy imparted by ionizing radiation per unit mass of irradiated material. The unit of absorbed dose is the rad.

(2) *Activity*. The rate of disintegration (transformation) or decay of radioactive material. The unit of activity is the curie.

(3) *Adult*. An adult is an individual 18 years of age or older.

(4) *Airborne Radioactivity Area*. A room, enclosure or area in which airborne radioactive materials exist in concentrations in excess of the derived air concentrations (DACs) specified in Table I, Column 3 of Appendix B, Title 10 Part 20 of the Code of Federal Regulations, or concentrations so an individual present in the area without respiratory protective equipment could exceed, during the hours the individual is present in a week, an intake of 0.6 percent of the annual limit on intake (ALI).

(5) *Annual Limit on Intake (ALI)*. The Annual Limit on Intake (ALI) of radioactive materials is the smaller amount of radioactive material taken into the body of an adult worker by inhalation or ingestion in a year (40 hours per week for 50 weeks) that would result in: a committed effective dose equivalent of 5 rem (0.05 Sv) or a committed dose equivalent of 50 rem (0.5 Sv) to any individual organ or tissue. The ALI values are based on the intake rate and standards for "reference man" as defined in International Commission on Radiological Protection Report No. 23, 1975.

(6) *Background Radiation*. Background radiation is radiation from cosmic sources; naturally occurring radioactive materials, including radon in concentrations or levels commonly found in structures or the environment; and global fallout as it commonly exists in the environment from the testing of nuclear explosive devices. Background radiation does not include radiation from source, byproduct, or special nuclear materials regulated by the Nuclear Regulatory Commission.

(7) *Calendar Quarter*. A calendar quarter is a period of time not less than 12 consecutive weeks nor more than 14 consecutive weeks. The first calendar quarter shall begin in January or begin with the dosimetry issue cycle closest to January. Subsequent calendar quarters shall begin within 12 to 14 weeks of that date so no day is included in both quarters or omitted from either quarter.

(8) *Committed Dose Equivalent* ($H_T,50$). Committed Dose Equivalent is the dose equivalent to an organ or tissue that will be received from an intake of radioactive material by an individual during the 50 year period following the intake, i.e., 50 year organ dose (total dose for 50 years from internal contamination).

(9) *Committed Effective Dose Equivalent* ($H_E,50$). Committed Effective Dose Equivalent is the sum of the products of the weighting factors applicable to each of the body organs or tissues that are irradiated and the committed dose equivalent to these organs or tissues. ($H_E,50 = \Sigma \ w_T H_T,50$; see weighting factor table for w_T values).

(10) *Controlled Area*. Controlled area is an area outside a restricted area but inside the site boundary, access to which can be limited by the activity for any reason.

(11) *Curie (Ci)*. The unit of radioactivity. One curie equals 3.7×10^{10} nuclear disintegrations per second. (1 Ci = 3.7×10^{10} Becquerel)

(12) *Declared Pregnant Woman*. A woman who has voluntarily informed her employer, in writing, of her pregnancy and the estimated date of conception.

(13) *Deep Dose Equivalent* (H_d). Deep dose equivalent, which applies to external whole-body exposure, is the dose equivalent at a tissue depth of 1 cm (1000 mg/cm^2). Deep dose equivalent establishes a standard depth for specifying the dose from whole body external exposure.

(14) *Derived Air Concentration (DAC)*. Derived air concentration is the concentration of a given radionuclide in air which, if breathed by the "reference man" for a working year (40 hours per week for 50 weeks) under conditions of light work (inhalation rate 1.2 cubic meters of air per hour), results in an intake of one ALI.

(15) *Dose*. A generic term that means absorbed dose, dose equivalent, effective dose equivalent, committed dose equivalent,

committed effective dose equivalent or total effective dose equivalent.

(16) *Dose Equivalent (H$_T$)*. The product of the absorbed dose (D) and the quality factor (Q), where H$_T$=DQ. Its purpose is to have a single unit, regardless of the type of radiation, describing the radiation effect on man. The dose equivalent has the unit "rem." The dose equivalent for each type and energy of ionizing radiation shall be determined by using the following quality factors or neutron fluences unless otherwise approved by BUMED.

(a) For x-ray, gamma or beta radiation, the quality factor will be equal to one.

(b) For neutrons of unknown energy and for protons, the quality factor will be equal to 10.

(c) For neutron fluences with known energy distributions, the dose equivalent will be determined using the table of Neutron Fluence per Unit Dose Equivalents in Title 10, Part 20 of the Code of Federal Regulations.

(d) For ionizing particles heavier than protons and with sufficient energy to reach the lens of the eye, the quality factor will be equal to 20.

(17) *Effective Dose Equivalent (H$_E$)*. The probability of a stochastic effect, e.g., cancer induction or heredity effect, in any tissue is proportional to the dose equivalent to that tissue. The value for the proportionality factors differs among the various tissues because of the differences in tissue sensitivity. If radiation dose is uniform throughout the body then the total risk factor is one. For non-uniform radiation, such as partial body exposure to an external radiation field, or from internal exposure where the isotope concentrates to different degrees in the various tissues, weighting factors which are based on the relative susceptibility of the tissues to stochastic effects may be used to calculate an effective dose equivalent. The effective dose equivalent is the sum of the products of the weighting factors applicable to each of the body organs or tissues that are irradiated and the dose equivalent to these organs or tissues. (H$_E$ = Σ w$_T$H$_T$, see weighting factor table under the definition of weighting factor for w$_T$ values).

(18) *Exposure*. Being exposed to ionizing radiation or to radioactive material.

(19) *External Personnel Contamination*. An area of the body is considered to be externally contaminated if it contains in excess of 450 picocuries of beta-gamma emitters by direct frisk or 50 picocuries of alpha emitting contamination by direct frisk, i.e., 100 counts/minute above background of beta-gamma emitting contamination (Cobalt-60 equivalent) as measured under the area of a DT-304 probe or 50 counts/minute above background of alpha emitting contamination as measured on an AN/PDR-56 with small probe. Different limits may be approved by the Naval Radiation Safety Committee for radioactive material used under a Naval Radioactive Material Permit or by Chief, BUMED for radioactive material not under a Naval Radioactive Material Permit.

(20) *Extremities*. Extremities means hand, elbow, arm below the elbow, foot, knee, or leg below the knee.

(21) *Eye Dose Equivalent*. Eye Dose Equivalent applies to the external exposure of the lens of the eye and is taken as the dose equivalent at a tissue depth of 0.3 centimeter.

(22) *High Radiation Area*. Any radiation area accessible to personnel in which there exists ionizing radiation at such levels an individual could receive in excess of 100 mrem (1 mSv) in 1 hour at 30 centimeters (approximately 1 foot) from the radiation source or from any surface the radiation penetrates.

(23) *Ionizing Radiation*. Any electromagnetic or particulate radiation capable of producing ions, directly or indirectly, in its passage through matter. Ionizing radiation includes the following: gamma rays, x-rays, alpha particles, beta particles, neutrons, protons, and other particles and electromagnetic waves capable of producing ions.

(24) *Ionizing Radiation Sources*. Any material, equipment or device which emits or is capable of generating ionizing radiation. This includes naturally occurring and artificially induced radioactive material; special nuclear material; nuclear reactors, particle generators and accelerators; medical or dental x-ray or fluoroscopic equipment; industrial radiographic equipment; certain electromagnetic wave generators; and certain analytical instruments such as x-ray diffraction spectrometers, electron microscopes, nuclear moisture density meters, etc.

(25) *Members of the Public*. Individuals who are not occupationally exposed to ionizing radiation shall be considered members of the public. Examples would include individuals that live and work outside the perimeter of a base or activity, family members of an employee or crew member that live on a base but are outside a controlled industrial area, and visitors that do not normally receive occupational exposure.

(26) *Minimum Detectable Activity (MDA)*. The minimum detectable activity is the amount of a radionuclide, if present in a sample, that would be detected with a 5 percent probability of non-detection, while accepting a probability of 5 percent of erroneously detecting that radionuclide in an appropriate blank sample. Minimum detectable activity is the minimum amount of radioactivity that can be detected at the 95 percent confidence level.

(27) *Non-ionizing Radiation*. Any electromagnetic radiation, including ultraviolet, visible, or infrared light, radio or microwaves, or laser radiation, which generally does not produce ionizations in its interaction with matter.

(28) *Non-stochastic Effect*. Non-stochastic effect means health effects, the severity of which varies with the dose and for which a threshold is believed to exist. Radiation induced cataract formation is an example of a non-stochastic effect.

(29) *Non-radiation Workers*. Non-radiation workers are employees or crew members who may receive very low level radiation exposure incidental to their employment at a command or activity but not as an integral part of their skill, trade or work assignment.

(30) *Occupationally Exposed Personnel.* Occupationally exposed personnel are individuals that receive exposure to ionizing radiation in the course of their employment or duties. Occupationally exposed personnel include both radiation workers and non-radiation workers.

(31) *Quality Factor (Q).* That factor which is multiplied by the absorbed dose (D) to obtain a quantity which equates to a common scale, the dose equivalent (H_T), of any type of ionizing radiation to which an individual is exposed ($H_T = DQ$).

(32) *Rad (rad).* The unit of absorbed dose (D) which is equal to the absorption of 100 ergs per gram.

(33) *Radiation Area.* Any area to which access shall be limited as deemed necessary by the cognizant authority and in which appropriate precautionary measures are taken to protect personnel from exposure to radiation or radioactive material. A "radiation area" includes any area accessible to personnel in which there exists ionizing radiation at dose-rate levels so that an individual could receive a deep dose equivalent in excess of 5 mrem (0.05 mSv) in 1 hour at 30 centimeters from the radiation source or from any surface that the radiation penetrates.

(34) *Radiation Health Officer.* A Medical Department Officer or civilian who is qualified by virtue of education, training and/or professional experience, to supervise a radiation health program. The officer will normally function within the medical department of a ship or station and will normally not be assigned responsibilities in radiological controls/radiation safety except within BUMED activities. On ships without Medical Service Corps or Medical Corps officers attached, the senior enlisted medical department representative assigned radiation health duties shall be designated the radiation health officer. The radiation health officer shall plan, supervise, and administer the radiation health program.

(35) *Radiation Health Program.* A medical department responsibility comprising all methods and procedures designed to maintain and protect the health of personnel exposed to ionizing radiation or radioactive contamination. It includes, but is not necessarily limited to the following:

(a) Detecting and identifying radiation and contamination hazards.

(b) Determining, evaluating and documenting personnel exposures (both internal and external).

(c) Performing medical qualification and surveillance examinations of radiation workers before, after and during periods of employment involving occupational radiation exposure.

(d) Evaluating environmental monitoring and radiation control procedures related to radiation health.

(e) Reviewing training and qualification requirements of personnel handling radioactive material, or working in radiation areas, as applicable to radiation health.

(f) Conducting radiation health training for involved personnel as necessary.

(g) Ensuring compliance with BUMED and other relevant instructions in the area of radiation health.

(h) Submitting required reports and maintaining applicable records.

(i) Assisting, as required, in the radiation health aspects of nuclear accident preparedness, CBR warfare defense, and disaster control planning.

(j) Promoting a high state of awareness and compliance with radiation health precepts.

(36) *Radiation Workers.* Radiation workers are individuals who receive exposure to ionizing radiation in the course of their employment or duties and are identified by their command as being occupationally exposed. Normally, these individuals' routine duties require working directly with sources of ionizing radiation and have a significant potential for exposure. These individuals receive radiation medical examinations. These individuals normally receive specialized training as part of a specific radiological controls program.

(37) *Radioactive Contamination.* A radioactive substance dispersed in or on materials or places where it is undesirable. Unless a different limit is approved by the Naval Radiation Safety Committee for radioactive material used under a Naval Radioactive Material Permit, or by the Chief, Bureau of Medicine and Surgery for radioactive material not under a Naval Radioactive Material Permit, an object or area is considered to be contaminated when:

(a) The loose surface radioactivity exceeds 450 picocuries (450 micromicrocuries or 16.6 becquerel) of beta-gamma activity as measured on a dry filter paper wiped over an area of approximately 100 square centimeters.

(b) The loose surface radioactivity exceeds 50 picocuries (50 micromicrocuries or 1.85 becquerel) of alpha activity as measured on a dry filter paper wiped over an area of approximately 100 square centimeters.

(38) *Radiological Controls Program.* A command responsibility comprising all procedures and techniques which are used to control radiation sources and radioactive material to minimize exposure to personnel and the environment. It includes control of all ionizing radiation sources during storage, handling, use, shipping and disposal.

(39) *Radiological Controls/Radiation Safety Officer.* An individual who shall be appointed by the unit commander to provide consultation and advice regarding the implementation of controls for the hazards associated with radiation sources and the effectiveness of these measures. The individual shall be responsible to the unit commander for promulgating and supervising the radiological controls/radiation safety program. The individual is directly responsible for adequate and effective controls which prevent spread of contamination and exposure of personnel. This individual shall be technically qualified by virtue of education, training and/or professional experience to supervise the storage, issue, use and disposition of radioactive sources and shall have a thorough knowledge of applicable regulations pertaining to the control of radiation sources and radioactive material prior to appointment.

(40) REAB. The Radiation Effects Advisory Board reviews and determines an individual's

fitness for radiation work as described in BUMEDINST 6470.21 series.

(41) *Rem (rem)*. The unit of dose equivalent(H_T) which is equal to the absorbed dose in rad multiplied by the quality factor. The rem shall be the unit of dose equivalent for record purposes unless otherwise specified by BUMED.

(42) *Restricted Area*. Restricted area means an area, access to which is limited by the Command for the purpose of protecting individuals against undue risks from exposure to radiation and radioactive materials. Restricted Areas may not include areas used as residential quarters, but separate rooms in a residential building may be set apart as a restricted area.

(43) *Roentgen (R)*. A unit of exposure to ionizing radiation. It is that amount of x-ray or gamma radiation which will produce in air 2.58×10^{-4} coulombs of charge per kilogram of air.

(44) *Shallow Dose Equivalent (H_S)*. Shallow Dose Equivalent, which applies to the external exposure of the skin or an extremity, is taken as the dose equivalent at a tissue depth of 0.007 centimeter (7 mg/cm^2) (average depth of the germinal cell layer of the skin) averaged over an area of 1 square centimeter.

(45) *Stochastic Effects*. Stochastic effects means health effects that occur randomly and for which the probability of the effect occurring, rather than its severity, is assumed to be a linear function of dose without threshold. Hereditary effects and cancer incidence are examples of stochastic effects.

(46) *System International (SI) Units*. These units have been established by the International Commission on Radiation Units and Measurements (ICRU) and are used by many countries. As such, they may be encountered in the scientific literature. These units compare to the rem, rad and curie, referred to as "traditional units" in the following manner:

One gray (Gy) = 100 rad
One sievert (Sv) = 100 rem
One becquerel (Bq) = 2.7×10^{-11} curie (Ci)
= One disintegration/sec.
One rad = One centigray (cGy)
= 1×10^{-2} gray (Gy)
One rem = One centisievert (cSv)
= 1×10^{-2} sievert (Sv)
One curie = 3.7×10^{10} becquerel (Bq)

(47) *Total Effective Dose Equivalent*. Total Effective Dose Equivalent is the sum of the deep dose equivalent (external dose) and the committed effective dose equivalent (internal dose).

(48) *Unrestricted Areas*. Any area to which access is neither limited or controlled by the activity and any area used for residential quarters.

(49) *Very High Radiation Area*. Any area accessible to personnel in which there exists ionizing radiation at such levels that an individual could receive in excess of 500 rads (5 grays) in 1 hour at 1 meter from the radiation source or from any surface that the radiation penetrates. Note: At very high doses received at high dose rates, units of absorbed dose (e.g., rad and gray) are appropriate, rather than units of dose equivalent (e.g., rem and sievert).

(50) *Weighting Factors (W_T)*. The weighting factor for an organ or tissue is the proportion of the risk of stochastic effects (random probability effects, e.g., cancer) resulting from irradiation of that organ or tissue to the total risk of stochastic effects when the whole body is irradiated uniformly. For calculating the effective dose equivalent, the values are:

ORGAN DOSE WEIGHTING FACTORS

Organ or Tissue	Factor
Gonads	0.25
Breast	0.15
Red bone marrow	0.12
Lung	0.12
Thyroid	0.03
Bone surfaces	0.03
Remainder*	0.30
Whole Body	1.00

* 0.30 results from 0.06 for each of 5 "remainder" organs (excluding the skin and lens of the eye) that receive the highest doses. The individual sections of the GI tract, i.e., stomach, small intestine, upper large intestine, and lower large intestine, are treated as individual organs.

(51) *Whole Body*. Whole body means, for purposes of external exposure, head, trunk (including male gonads), arms above the elbow, and legs above the knee.

1-6. Radiation Health Program Evaluation

(1) To ensure compliance with regulations and procedures specified in this manual, evaluations of the Radiation Health Program shall be conducted as follows:

(a) For forces afloat and intermediate maintenance activities audited under type commander (TYCOM) directives, an audit shall be conducted at least annually by medical department personnel from group, squadron, or type commanders, e.g., squadron medical officers, squadron hospital corpsmen, radiation health officers, etc. For nuclear-powered ships, the ship's executive officer shall also be a member of the audit team. The executive officer's participation qualifies this audit as one of the semiannual radiation health audits required by OPNAVINST C9210-2 series (Engineering Department Manual for Naval Nuclear Propulsion Plants).

(b) For shore stations, two audits per year (conducted approximately 6 months apart) shall be conducted by personnel knowledgeable in radiation health, but who are as independent as possible of the local radiation health program.

(c) For naval shipyards with large radiation health programs, BUMED performs periodic audits. The BUMED audits are in addition to the audits required by paragraph 1-6(1)(b), and shall not be used to replace them.

(2) When performing medical record reviews in conjunction with evaluations of radiation health programs, auditors should focus only on findings that affect the physical qualification of the individual to

receive occupational radiation exposure (i.e., the technical aspects of the physical examination). Other findings that are only administrative in nature, such as date and name formatting errors and eyesight and dental data transcription errors, should be identified to the command, but shall not be cited as radiation health record deficiencies.

(3) A copy of the audit report shall be retained and be available for review for a period of 3 years.

Chapter 2
MEDICAL EXAMINATIONS

2-1. Introduction

(1) Personnel occupational radiation exposure criteria are based upon the concept there may be some degree of risk from any level of radiation exposure, although medical knowledge shows the risk from radiation exposure within limits to be small. No radiation injuries have been documented in man for exposures which were compliant with existing radiation protection guides.

(2) Radiation workers receive medical examinations to establish baseline results and evaluate disease states which may medically disqualify a person from receiving occupational radiation exposure.

(3) The medical standards are based on:

(a) The radiation worker accepting some small degree of risk which is balanced against benefits, based upon competent technical appraisal.

(b) A deliberate selection of radiation worker candidates.

(4) Ionizing radiation medical examinations are documented on two forms: (1) Report of Medical Examination (SF-88) and (2) Report of Medical History (SF-93). The Department of Defense is in the process of replacing these forms with analogous forms; DD Form 2808 and DD Form 2807.1, respectively. Until BUMED authorizes the DD forms for this specific usage, the SF-88 and SF-93 shall continue to be used to document ionizing radiation medical examinations.

2-2. Types of Ionizing Radiation Medical Examinations

(1) *Preplacement Examination (PE)*.

(a) All personnel who are being considered for assignment as radiation workers will be given an ionizing radiation medical examination, defined as a preplacement examination (PE), prior to assignment or transfer to those duties. This includes individuals who have been radiation workers at one time or another, received a termination examination and are now being considered for reentry into the program.

(b) Non-radiation workers and members of the general public, are not required to have a PE.

(c) Visitors including messengers, servicemen, and delivery men, are not required to have a PE.

(d) Emergency response personnel; dentists, dental technicians and other dental paraprofessionals; nurses and ward personnel; explosive ordinance disposal team members; and certain crew members or employees whose exposure is truly sporadic, are not required to have a PE. (See appropriate radiological controls manuals for specific program requirements.)

(e) Individuals who are not required to have a PE but who exceed 500 mrem (5 mSv) exposure in a calendar year, must have a PE within 1 month of the time they exceed 500 mrem (5 mSv) or as soon thereafter as operational requirements permit.

(2) *Reexamination (RE)*. Personnel who are to be continued in routine duties as radiation workers must have an ionizing radiation medical examination, defined as a reexamination (RE), as follows: Periodicity between examinations will not exceed 5 years up to age 50. After age 50 examinations are required every 2 years, e.g., an individual examined at age 46 would be re-examined at 51, an individual examined at age 47, 48, 49 or 50 would be reexamined at age 52. Beginning at age 60 the examination is required annually. (See Manual of the Medical Department (MANMED) Chapter 15.) The examination may be performed earlier than the required frequency for the purpose of even distribution of medical examination workload, or to combine the reexamination with a medical examination required for another purpose, or for any other reason. The RE is required to be performed no later than one month following the anniversary date (month and year) of the previous radiation medical examination or other medical examination accepted and documented as a radiation medical examination, e.g., for an examination performed on the 15th of February 1985, the reexamination must be completed by 31 March 1990. When constrained by ship operating schedules, the examination is to be performed at the earliest opportunity.

(3) *Situational Examination (SE)*. Any individual who has exceeded the radiation protection standards for radiation workers as stated in Chapter 4, or has ingested or inhaled a quantity of radioactive material exceeding 50 percent of an annual limit of intake (ALI), or as deemed necessary by the responsible medical officer must be given an ionizing radiation medical examination, defined as a situational examination (SE). ALIs are listed in International Commission on Radiological Protection, Publication Number 30 or in Appendix B of Title 10, Part 20. ALIs for commonly used isotopes are reprinted for convenience in Appendix B of this manual. The medical history must contain summary statements which provide the basis for performing the examination.

(4) *Termination Examination (TE)*. Reasonable efforts will be made to ensure a radiation worker receives a

termination examination (TE). If a TE is not completed or not performed, e.g., due to lack of employee cooperation, etc., a Form SF-88 will be prepared and completed to the maximum extent practicable. The reasons why the form is incomplete will be recorded in the disqualifying defects block of the SF-88. Radiation workers will be given a TE as near as practical to but no earlier than 6 months prior to satisfying one of the following conditions:

(a) Upon separation or termination of their active duty or employment if they received a PE and have documented occupational radiation exposure (including personnel monitored for exposure but who received 00.000 rem).

(b) When permanently removed from the radiation health program.

(c) When permanently removed from duties as a radiation worker.

(5) *Other Examinations.* Medical examinations other than radiation medical examinations and results of consultations for individuals physically qualified as radiation workers will be reviewed by a medical officer or medical department representative for findings or evaluations affecting continued qualifications as a radiation worker. The scope of other medical examinations need not be expanded to cover the requirements of this article unless the examination is to be used as a radiation medical examination. Medical examinations performed outside the Department of Defense are not to be requested for routine review. Individuals may submit medical information from their private physicians for consideration by the responsible medical officer. In these cases, the Navy remains solely responsible for determining whether the medical information from the private physician will be accepted or rejected.

2-3. Scope of Examination

(1) The examination for active duty members shall include the additional requirements of the routine active duty examination. Examinations for civilian personnel are only required to include the items specific to employment under Office of Personnel Management regulations and those listed here.

(2) The medical examination will place particular emphasis on determining the existence of malignant and premalignant lesions and other conditions which could be related to radiation exposure. A medical officer with knowledge of the potential biological effects of ionizing radiation will review any medical history or presence of disease states or abnormalities related to the following: history of occupational exposure to ionizing radiation in excess of that allowed by current directives; history of radiation therapy; and, medical conditions which may be associated with exposure to ionizing radiation. The radiation medical examination will include, but not be limited to, a careful medical history, physical examination, complete blood count, urinalysis and other clinical laboratory studies or procedures, and bioassays, as indicated.

(a) *Medical History.* A complete medical history on the SF-93 will be obtained, including all changes in medical history since the last radiation health examination. Medical histories will include:

(1) History of accidental or occupational exposure to ionizing radiation above Table III limits;

(2) History of cancer or precancerous lesions;

(3) History of anemia;

(4) History of radiation therapy;

(5) History of radiopharmaceutical received for therapeutic or experimental purposes;

(6) History of work involving the handling of unsealed radium sources or other unsealed sources.

(b) *Medical Examination.* The examination will consist of the items described in the clinical evaluation blocks of the SF-88 with the following modifications for civilian personnel:

(1) Female pelvic examination is not required. Breast examinations are required for females age 36 or older. The digital rectal examination is only required for male examinees age 36 or older. For personnel who are less than 36 the above examinations may be offered but are not required.

(c) *Special Studies.* The required special studies are a CBC and a urinalysis. In addition, the following special studies may apply:

(1) Internal Monitoring. All personnel assigned to duties involving the handling of radioactive material in a form so that they could reasonably be expected to exceed 10 percent of an annual limit on intake (ALI) in 1 year through inhalation, ingestion or absorption will be evaluated for evidence of a partial body burden before and after assignment to such duties, e.g., at the start and completion of a tour involving these duties. Periodic monitoring will be conducted as deemed necessary by the responsible medical officer or radiation health officer. Additional requirements to perform internal monitoring due to specific work environments will be issued in applicable program radiological controls manuals with Chief, BUMED concurrence or as conditions of radioactive material permits.

(2) Radon Breath Analysis or Radium Urine Bioassay. All personnel assigned to duties involving the handling of radium, or its compounds, not hermetically sealed so that they could reasonably be expected to receive 10 percent of an annual limit on intake (ALI) in 1 year will have radon breath analysis or radium urine bioassay at the beginning and end of such assignment or following personnel contamination incidents involving loose surface contamination of radium compounds such that the individual could have received 10 percent of an ALI. Chapter 3 provides guidance for obtaining a radon breath

analysis or radium urine bioassay. Other methods of determining internal radium deposition may be used if approved by Chief, BUMED.

(3) Bioassay. When deemed necessary by the responsible medical officer or radiation health officer bioassay may be performed on body tissues, secretions, and excretions to estimate an exposure from internal contaminates. If a command lacks the capability to perform appropriate bioassay, a request will be submitted to one of the support facilities designated in Chapter 3.

(4) Additional requirements to perform special examinations due to specific work environments can be provided in the applicable program radiological controls manual with Chief, BUMED approval.

2-4. Standards

(1) The general requirements are those for active duty in the military service or in civil service employment, as amended by this article. Individuals found not physically qualified based upon these requirements may be reevaluated at a later date. The following will be cause for rejection or disqualification unless the condition is reviewed and the individual found qualified for radiation work by the BUMED Radiation Effects Advisory Board (REAB) (refer to Article 2-7):

(a) History of cancer.

(b) History of radiation therapy which may have compromised bone marrow reserves.

(c) History of polycythemia vera.

(d) Cancerous or precancerous lesions. Exceptions: Adequately treated actinic keratosis, basal cell carcinoma, and abnormal PAP smear are not disqualifying.

(e) Open lesions or wounds (including lacerations, abrasions, and ulcerative, eruptive, or exfoliative lesions). These are disqualifying either on a temporary or permanent basis, depending on the condition, for individuals who handle radioactive material which is not hermetically sealed, until such time as the medical department representative or medical officer considers the wound to be adequately protected from radioactive contamination.

(f) Abnormal Blood count:

(1) Any deviation of the complete blood count (CBC) outside laboratory normal values or the values in Table I if manually performed must be evaluated by a medical officer and a determination made whether the individual is considered disqualified (CD) or not considered disqualified (NCD). The basis for a determination of CD/NCD must be given by the responsible medical officer as a comment in the summary of defects and diagnosis block.

(2) CBC values, manual or automated, which persist outside the ranges in Table II will be considered disqualifying until review by the BUMED REAB. The medical officer's evaluation of the CBC and his/her requests for other studies or consultations must be directed toward the determination of malignant or premalignant conditions and hematopoietic system reserve.

(3) Differential white blood cell count is required when the WBC is outside laboratory normal or Table I values as applicable. The differential shall be evaluated for any gross cell count anomalies. Minor deviations from the normal range which are not indicative of a cancerous or precancerous condition are not considered disqualifying; however, all differential WBC counts outside the normal range require comment in the summary of defects and diagnosis block of the SF-88 with a determination of CD or NCD.

TABLE I
Complete Blood Count Parameters

There are two acceptable laboratory methods for determining blood count parameters, manual and automated machine.

Blood Parameter	Male	Female
Hematocrit (Hct)	40-52%	37-47%
Hemoglobin (Hgb) (optional)	14-18g/dl	12-16g/dl
White Blood Count (WBC)	4,000-12,000/cubic mm	

Differential Count

Manual	Male & Female
Neutrophils (N)	40-80%
Lymphocytes (L)	20-50%
Bands (BF)	0-10%
Eosinophils (E)	0-10%
Basophils (B)	0-3%
Monocytes (M)	0-10%
Atypical Lymphocytes (ATL)	0-10%

Some automated machines will provide differential counts that categorize the white blood cells (leukocytes) by the traditional manual leukocyte classification, as above. Other machines may use other classifications, which are as acceptable for diagnosis and prognosis, for example:

Automated	
Lymphocytes	20.5-51.1%
Monocytes	0.0-9.3%
Granulocytes (Neutrophils)	42.2-75.1%
Large unstained cells	less than 4%

Any clinically acceptable automated differential white blood count method suffices for the needs of the radiation health program. However, if the automated machine categorization differs from those provided above, the laboratory data sheet must be filed in the health record or the normal ranges for the machine must be recorded along with the results of the study on the SF-88.

TABLE II

	Male & Female
Hematocrit	35-56%
Hemoglobin (optional)	11g/dl-19g/dl
White Blood Count	3,500-14,000/cubic mm

(g) Urinalysis. Urine will be tested for red blood cells using either a standard clinical dipstick method or microscopic high power field. Document the results of red blood cell testing in the "microscopic" block of the physical examination form. Repeat testing for positive results must be performed by high power field. Red blood cells in the urine (greater than 5 RBCs per high power field) persisting on repeat urinalysis will be considered disqualifying, pending definitive determination of other than a malignant condition. Other abnormal urinalysis results may be of clinical significance (e.g., low specific gravity, positive sugar or albumin, WBCs or casts) dictating follow-up evaluation at the discretion of the examiner; however, they are not in themselves disqualifying for occupational exposure to ionizing radiation. Nonetheless, all abnormal urinalysis findings require comment in the SF-88 Summary of Defects and Diagnosis block and a determination of CD or NCD.

(h) If an individual has internally deposited radionuclides associated with an intake of 50 percent of an ALI or more in 1 year the individual shall be disqualified from duties involving occupational radiation exposure pending BUMED review. ALI values for some common isotopes are provided in Appendix B.

(i) Other defects which pose a health or safety hazard to the individual, co-workers, or degrade the safety of the work-place.

2-5. Special Documentation Requirements

(1) The following specific requirements will be adhered to in addition to the requirements for completing the Standard Form 88 and 93 as listed in Chapters 15 and 16 of the Manual of the Medical Department. Local reproduction of these forms and computer-generated SF-88 and SF-93 forms are authorized; however, these forms must have all the required technical information. Example forms are provided in Appendix A.

(a) Use of an overprint or rubber stamp on the SF-93 for the required supplemental history questions is acceptable. Instructions in the hospitalization blocks of the SF-93 require certain additional information be provided for a "positive answer," for the purpose of radiation medical examinations, the name of the doctor, clinic or hospital is not needed.

(b) All radiation medical examinations require a medical officer's signature in the reviewing officer block of the SF-88. This medical officer is responsible for reviewing the complete medical examination including laboratory and other information to determine qualification. The reviewing medical officer may be the same as the examining medical officer. The SF-88 reviewing officer block entry will include the date of final review in the margin immediately below the signature of the reviewing official.

(c) The medical history will be signed by the examining medical officer.

(d) Records of medical examination (SF-88 and SF-93) performed by a physician assistant or nurse practitioner must be countersigned by a physician.

(e) For the summary of defects and diagnosis block of the SF-88 and the physician's summary block of the SF-93 any entry concerning an abnormal finding will have an indication of "NCD" or "CD" per MANMED Chapter 15.

(f) For the purpose of a radiation medical examination, the term "Essentially Negative" or "ESS. NEG." has the same meaning as "Negative."

(g) Non-completion of a radiation medical examination must be documented in the notes block of the SF-88 with specific reasons for non-completion.

(h) Radiation medical examinations will clearly state whether the individual is physically qualified (PQ) or not physically qualified (NPQ) for ionizing radiation work.

(i) The fact that a termination medical examination is required will be entered on the front of the individual's health record jacket or employee medical file as "Termination Radiation Medical Examination Required."

(j) Medical examinations conducted for a purpose other than ionizing radiation work may be amended per MANMED Chapter 15 and Article 2-6 at the discretion of the responsible medical officer. If a previous medical examination is accepted, the date of the required reexamination will be based on the original date (month and year) of the accepted examination.

(k) Results of bioassay, internal monitoring, etc., which document monitoring for internally deposited radioactivity, will be documented as required in Chapter 5.

(l) Consultative reports from specialists shall be recorded on the SF-513, or on letterhead stationery if the specialist is not a government health care provider.

(m) No radiation medical examination report or portion thereof shall be removed from an individual's health record.

2-6. Validity Periods and Correction of Deficient Examinations

(1) A medical examination conducted for another purpose may be upgraded to a radiation medical examination and will be valid until the next required medical examination (see Article 2-2(2) and MANMED Chapter 15), provided there has been no significant change in the member's physical condition, and the examination is of the proper clinical scope. Examinations are considered deficient in scope when clinical evaluations unique to the examination are missing or incomplete.

(a) If more than 90 days has elapsed the examination must be upgraded by an interview with a medical officer or credentialed provider to include, at a minimum, a review of health record, interval history, and applicable special studies.

(1) If the examination is sufficient in clinical scope to meet the requirements of a radiation medical examination, then a statement of the additional purpose and interval history (e.g., "Member examined this date, no significant interval history noted. PQ for Ionizing Radiation Work") will be made in the notes block of the SF-88 and signed and dated by the reviewing physician.

(2) If the examination is deficient in clinical scope, the appropriate clinical studies and procedures will be performed which satisfy the additional requirements. This information will be added to the above statement in the notes block of the SF-88.

(b) If there is insufficient space in the notes block of the SF-88, then an addendum SF-88 will be prepared. The following entry must be made in the bottom margin on the front of the SF-88; "Addendum to Medical Examination dated _____." The following blocks; name, grade and component, identification number, purpose of examination, dates of examination, qualification block, and typed or printed name of the reviewing officer, and appropriate blocks for information being added will be completed on the addendum SF-88. Other blocks on the addendum SF-88 may be left blank. The purpose of the examination block and the qualification block must indicate the new purpose of examination (e.g., Ionizing Radiation Work (RE)).

(c) The addendum SF-88 will be filed immediately behind the original SF-88 and number of attached sheets, if any, to the original SF-88 will be indicated in the space provided opposite the reviewing officer block.

(d) If a previous medical examination is accepted by the cognizant examiner, the date of the next required radiation examination will be based on the date of the original accepted examination.

(2) The SF-93 may be corrected in a fashion similar to that described above, using the physician's summary block for the additional information, if considered appropriate by the examining or reviewing medical officer. If an addendum SF-93 is required, the following blocks; name, identification number, purpose of examination, date of examination, individual's signature and date, typed or printed name of examiner, date and examiner's signature, and appropriate blocks for the required information will be completed. Block 5 must indicate the new purpose of examination (e.g., ionizing radiation work (RE)). The following entry must be made in the bottom margin on the front of the SF-93; "Addendum to Medical History dated _____."

(3) Administrative correction will be made as described in Chapter 16 of the Manual

of the Medical Department, i.e., single line drawn through erroneous entry, initialed, and corrected entry made. Corrected entries may be made in the Notes block of the SF-88, the physician's summary block of the SF-93, or on an addendum.

(4) Exception to the aforementioned validity period and correction procedures: Medical examination and health record entries will conform to the standards prescribed at the time of the examination, i.e., clinically upgrading or administratively correcting examinations which were conducted prior to implementing this change is not required.

2-7. Reporting Requirements for the REAB

(1) The following medical examinations and supporting medical documents (see Article 2-8) must be submitted to Chief, BUMED, Undersea Medicine and Radiation Health Division, for review by the Radiation Effects Advisory Board (REAB) per BUMEDINST 6470.21 series. The board will perform a review and determine the individual's fitness for radiation work. The transmittal letter must include the reason for submittal, total lifetime exposure of the individual, summary of the individual's duties, and if appropriate the current or disqualifying diagnosis. Only medical examinations which are completed and for which all required consultative results are available should be submitted for review.

(a) Findings on a radiation medical examination which disqualify an individual from ionizing radiation work.

(b) Findings on a medical history or medical examination of:

(1) History of ionizing radiation exposure or internal deposition in excess of that allowed by Articles 2-4 and 4-3(1)(a).

(2) History of radiation therapy.

(3) An intake in excess of 50 percent of an ALI of radioactive material not intentionally administered for medical diagnosis or treatment. A description of the analysis technique must be included with the submission.

(c) Any medical examination or condition which the responsible medical officer or commanding officer recommends for Chief, BUMED review. Such request for review will not be denied by any member of the chain of command.

(d) All SEs.

(e) Allegations or claim by a service member or employee that his/her physical condition was caused by exposure to ionizing radiation.

2-8. Documentation Requirements for the REAB

(1) All cases submitted to the BUMED REAB for review must include the most recent radiation medical examination and supporting medical documentation directly related to the individual's medical condition, including laboratory and special studies results, consultation reports, and any evaluations performed by the individual's private medical doctor.

(2) Cases submitted to the BUMED REAB for reconsideration of an individual previously found not physically qualified by the BUMED REAB due to a diagnosis of cancer must include a current radiation medical examination performed subsequent to the individual completing all prescribed treatment. Additionally, supporting medical documentation must include conclusions by the treating physician and oncologist that the individual is free of cancer with a good long-term prognosis. A discussion of the medical procedures and pathology reports that support this conclusion should be provided. Finally, the treating physician's or oncologist's follow-up plan to ensure the worker remains cancer-free should also be provided.

Chapter 3
SUPPORT FACILITIES

3-1   Introduction

(1) This chapter provides guidance for obtaining assistance from support facilities for the completion of certain items required by this manual or program radiological controls manuals that are not readily available at every activity that employs radiation workers. Specific documentation requirements with regard to recording results are contained elsewhere in this manual and program radiological controls manuals.

3-2. Bioassay

(1) When deemed necessary by the cognizant medical officer or radiation health officer of a ship, unit, or command which lacks facilities to perform such analysis, a request for a bioassay is to be submitted to the Naval Dosimetry Center, Navy Environmental Health Center Detachment, Bethesda, MD, 20889-5614. DSN 295-0142 or 295-5410 or Commercial (301) 295-0142 or 295-5410. The Naval Dosimetry Center's Plain Language Address for message traffic is NAVENVIRHLTHCEN DET BETHESDA MD. The request shall include a general description of the event or circumstance which produced the possible internal radioactive deposition, the probable radioisotopes present, the results of previous radiochemical analysis, and any other pertinent information.

(2) When it has been determined bioassay are needed, the support facility will instruct the requesting activity regarding the collection, preservation, volume and number of specimens required. The support facility will recommend the appropriate shipment procedures to be used, and will supply appropriate containers and preservatives, if necessary.

3-3. Radon Bioassay

(1) All workroom, storage room, control room, and breath samples shall be collected in sampling bags, and 24-hour urine samples in appropriate containers, obtained on request, from the Naval Dosimetry Center. The request for sampling bags, urine collection containers, and equipment shall specify the number and types of samples to be taken, and shall include the name and telephone number of the individual to contact for shipping information. Instructions concerning sample collection and equipment will be provided by the laboratory. All sampling bags, urine collection containers, and equipment shall be shipped to the facility specified by the Naval Dosimetry Center within a period of approximately 2 weeks after receipt.

3-4. Internal Monitoring (External Counting)

(1) Personnel shall have internal monitoring performed when deemed necessary by the cognizant medical officer or radiation health officer (see Chapter 2), and as required by program radiological controls manuals. Naval organizations lacking the capability to perform internal monitoring examinations may request internal monitoring services from the nearest BUMED approved naval organization capable of providing internal monitoring. BUMED approved facilities (organizations) include:
(a) Shipyards, tenders, and submarine bases which perform radioactive work associated with naval nuclear propulsion plants.
(b) Nuclear-powered surface ships and naval reactor prototypes.
(c) Naval Dosimetry Center, Navy Environmental Health Center Detachment, Bethesda, MD 20889-5614.
(d) Naval Medical Center, San Diego, CA 92134-5000.
(e) Naval Nuclear Power School, Goose Creek, SC 29445-6324.
(f) Other organizations specifically authorized by BUMED or required as a condition of a Radioactive Material Permit.

3-5. Assistance For Evaluation and Treatment of Irradiated or Contaminated Personnel

(1) Specific guidance for evaluation, monitoring, care and decontamin ion of personnel is available in BUMED Instruction 6470.10 series. Advice on the significance of abnormal findings and assistance in the evaluation of personnel suspected of exceeding radiation exposure limits due to external or internal radiation exposure is to be obtained from: BUMED, telephone DSN: 762-3444, Commercial: 202-762-3444; after working hours telephone DSN: 762-3211, Commercial: 202-762-3211.

Chapter 4
RADIATION PROTECTION STANDARDS

4-1. Introduction

(1) *General*. Every effort shall be made to maintain personnel radiation exposures as far below Navy radiation protection standards as practicable. Current Navy radiation protection standards are consistent with or more stringent than those of the Environmental Protection Agency, Nuclear Regulatory Commission and the Occupational Safety and Health Administration.

(2) *Scope*. The standards prescribed herein are adopted for the control of ionizing radiation exposure to personnel within the naval establishment during peacetime and noncombatant operations, and do not include radiation exposure of an individual incident to medical or dental diagnostic or therapeutic procedures or to exposure from background radiation. These standards do not apply after an attack in which nuclear weapons are used, for combat operations, or during war; however, the provisions of these regulations insofar as they are feasible, shall remain in effect. Any and all exceptions to the following standards must be approved by the Chief, Bureau of Medicine and Surgery.

4-2. Members of the Public

(1) Radioactive material and other sources of radiation shall not be used, maintained, or transferred in such a manner to cause:

(a) the dose in any unrestricted area, from external sources, to exceed 2 mrem (0.02 mSv) in any one hour.

(b) an individual member of the public to receive a total effective dose equivalent in excess of 100 mrem (1 mSv) in a calendar year, exclusive of the dose contribution from disposal of radioactive material into sanitary sewerage per a radioactive material permit.

(2) Exposure limits for members of the public shall continue to apply when the member enters a controlled area.

(3) Exposure limits for members of the public apply to unrestricted areas and berthing spaces.

(4) It must be locally documented, by measurement, calculation or both, that due to limited occupancy or transient situations:

(a) The maximum exposed individual's total effective dose equivalent from occupancy in all unrestricted areas would not be expected to exceed 100 mrem (1 mSv) per calendar year; or,

(b) The annual average concentrations of radioactive material released in gaseous and liquid effluents at the boundary of the unrestricted area do not exceed the values specified in Table 2 of Appendix B to Title 10 Part 20; and, if an individual were continually present in an unrestricted area, the dose from external sources would not exceed 2 mrem (0.02 mSv) in an hour and 50 mrem (0.5 mSv) in a year.

4-3. Occupational Exposures

(1) Radiation Workers.

(a) Radioactive material and/or other sources of radiation shall not be used in such a manner to cause an adult to receive the more conservative of the radiation doses specified in Table III.

TABLE III

Radiation Exposure Limits

Total Effective Dose Equivalent (Whole Body)	03.000 rem/qtr yr
Total Effective Dose Equivalent (Whole Body)	05.000 rem/yr
Shallow Dose Equivalent (Extremities)	50.000 rem/yr
Shallow Dose Equivalent (Skin)	50.000 rem/yr
Eye Dose Equivalent (Eyes)	15.000 rem/yr
Sum of Deep Dose Equivalent and Committed Dose Equivalent for any organ or tissue other than the Lens of the eye (Organ Dose)	50.000 rem/yr

(b) For radiation workers whose prior current year exposure is unknown, the annual limits shall be reduced by one-quarter for each quarter of the current year for which records of exposure are unavailable or incomplete. For example, if new employees are hired in June and state they were exposed at their previous job earlier in the year but records are unavailable, then the annual exposure limits for the new employees must be reduced by one-quarter for the first and second quarters of the year, i.e., reduced from 5 rem (0.05 Sv) to 2.5 rem (0.025 Sv), from 50 rem (0.5 Sv) to 25 rem (0.25 Sv) for shallow dose, 15 rem (0.15 Sv) to 7.5 rem (0.075 Sv) for eye dose and from 50 rem (0.5 Sv) to 25 rem (0.25 Sv) for the sum of deep dose equivalent and committed dose equivalent for any organ or tissue other than the lens of the eye.

(2) Nonradiation Workers. Radioactive material shall not be used in such a manner to cause any nonradiation worker to exceed a total effective dose equivalent of 500 mrem (5 mSv) per year considering occupancy factors and source usage. It must be locally documented that due to limited source usage, occupancy or transient situations the individual's total effective dose equivalent is not expected to exceed 500 mrem (5 mSv) per year.

4-4. Embryo/Fetus

(1) Once a woman monitored for occupational exposure notifies her command in writing of her pregnancy, exposure to the embryo/fetus shall not exceed 500 mrem (5 mSv) for the term of the pregnancy and shall not exceed 50 mrem (0.5 mSv) per month in any month for the remainder of the pregnancy.

(a) The dose to the embryo/fetus shall be taken as the sum of the deep dose equivalent to the declared pregnant woman and the dose to the embryo/fetus from radionuclides in the embryo/fetus and declared pregnant woman.

(b) If the dose to the embryo/fetus is found to have exceeded 500 mrem (5 mSv) or is within 50 mrem (0.5 mSv) of this dose, by the time the woman declares the pregnancy, the activity shall be deemed to be in compliance with the limit if the additional dose to embryo/fetus does not exceed 50 mrem (0.5 mSv) during the remainder of the pregnancy.

4-5. Minors

(1) No individual under 18 years of age shall receive an occupational exposure to ionizing radiation in excess of 10 percent of the exposure limits for radiation workers.

4-6. Emergency Exposure

(1) In an emergency it may be necessary for fire fighters or other workers to exceed limits prescribed in Table III to save life or valuable property. In such situations, the probable risk of high exposure to the rescuer must be weighed against the expected benefits. In emergency situations:

(a) Which require personnel to search for and remove injured personnel or which require entry to prevent conditions that would probably injure numbers of people, the planned total effective dose equivalent should not exceed 100 rem (1 Sv).

(b) Where it is desirable to enter a hazardous area to protect facilities, eliminate further escape of contamination, or to control fires, the planned total effective dose equivalent should not exceed 10 rem (0.1 Sv).

(c) The above emergency exposure guidance is based on criteria set forth in National Council on Radiation Protection and Measurements Reports Number 39 and 91. When an individual has been exposed to more than 3 rem (0.03 Sv) during the calendar quarter, or 5 rem (0.05 Sv) in a calendar year as a result of an emergency, he shall be restricted from any additional occupational exposure as a radiation worker to radiation pending BUMED review; and, his exposure shall be reported as an overexposure following the requirements of Chapter 5.

4-7. Radiation Protection Guidance for Internal Emitters

(1) If radioactive material is inhaled, ingested, or absorbed through the skin, it may be deposited in various organs or systems of the body. It then acts as a radiation source within the body and will continue to irradiate the cells of the body until it has been eliminated by biological processes and/or by radioactive decay. The amount of radioactive material retained in the body is limited by controlling the rate of intake of such material. This is accomplished primarily by limiting the concentration of radioactive materials on surfaces, in the air and water in the occupational environment. Risk of internal exposure is reduced by good housekeeping procedures, e.g., cleanliness, containment, protective clothing and appropriate exhaust ventilation.

(2) Intake of an ALI or exposure at the level of the DAC for 40 hours per week for a 50-week year should result in a committed effective dose equivalent of 5 rem (0.05 Sv) or 50 rem (0.5 Sv) to an organ or tissue, whichever is the more limiting. Appendix B lists ALIs, and DAC values which will result in an intake equal to an ALI for some of the isotopes used in the Navy. Tables of the ALI and DAC values for other radionuclides are published in Table I of Appendix B, Title 10, Part 20 of the Code of Federal Regulations.

(3) Personal protective measures may be accomplished by:

(a) Avoiding Inhalation.

(1) Personnel shall not work in an environment whenever 10 per cent of an annual limit on intake of radioactivity is likely to be exceeded without some action being taken to minimize the intake. Personnel shall not routinely work (2,000 hours expected) in an environment whenever 10 per cent of a DAC is likely to be exceeded without some action being taken to minimize the intake. Actions may include process or engineering controls, e.g., containment or ventilation, to minimize the concentration in the air or other controls, e.g., respirators, access control, limitation of exposure times, etc., to control and minimize the exposure of personnel.

(2) The commanding officer may authorize work without respiratory protection in environments where 10 per cent of a DAC may be exceeded for short periods of time, provided the exposure time during any 7 consecutive days is decreased proportionately from the 40-hour time limit. For example, if work is for 8 hours, the concentration levels may be 5 times 10 per cent of the DAC values listed in Appendix B of this manual or Table I of Appendix B, Title 10, Part 20 of the Code of Federal Regulations. Conversely, if a worker works more than 40 hours during any 7-consecutive day period and the number of hours of exposure is more than 40, the air concentration limits (DACs) shall be lowered proportionately. For example, if work is for

48 hours the air concentration values for work without respiratory protection are 5/6 of 10 per cent of those listed in Appendix B or Table I of Appendix B, Title 10, Part 20 of the Code of Federal Regulations.

(3) Personnel may work in an environment where 10 per cent of the DAC is expected to be exceeded provided the workers use respiratory equipment and protective clothing as appropriate; or, if the particle size and chemical or physical state of the radionuclide is so that it is unlikely that the workers will exceed 10 per cent of an ALI; or, if containments, glove bags, ventilation hoods or barriers are used such that 10 per cent of a DAC in the breathing zone is not likely to be exceeded.

(4) Respiratory protection from inhalation of radioisotopes is not required during decontamination or showering of a contaminated person unless it is expected the individual or the attendants will exceed 50 per cent of an ALI. Resuspension and redistribution factors may be used to calculate levels of activity necessary to pose a risk of exceeding 50 per cent of an ALI. (For cobalt 60, approximately 100 mCi would need to be present. This amount would give an external exposure rate of approximately 100 mrem (1 mSv) per hour at one meter from the contaminated person.)

(b) Avoiding ingestion. No edible material of any kind including chewing gum, candy, food, beverages, tobacco or smoking equipment shall be allowed in a contaminated area or stored in an area containing liquid or unsealed radioactive sources. Surface contamination levels will be minimized to preclude hand to mouth transfer of activity. Upon leaving a contaminated area personnel should not be permitted to handle edible materials until they have been carefully monitored and decontaminated if necessary.

(c) Avoiding absorption. Personnel should be provided, trained in the use of, and required to wear appropriate protective clothing in a contaminated area. Work surfaces (bench tops) where liquid radioactive material is used should be covered with absorbent paper or other material to minimize the potential for hand contact with any spilled liquid.

(4) If an individual receives an internal deposition or uptake of radionuclides determined by internal monitoring or bioassay as a result of his duties (occupational exposure), the committed effective dose equivalent will be calculated by a BUMED approved facility. (See Chapters 3 and 5.)

4-8. Radiation Protection Guidance for External Exposure

(1) When the source of ionizing radiation is located outside the body, the following methods of control are applicable:

(a) Time. Reducing an individual's working time in a radiation field is the simplest way to limit his exposure. Since the amount of radiation exposure received is equal to the dose rate multiplied by time of exposure, decreasing exposure time results in a proportional decrease in total exposure.

(b) Distance. Radiation intensity varies inversely as the square of the distance from a point source (i.e., a source concentrated in a small volume). Therefore, if a worker doubles the distance between himself and the source, his exposure is reduced to one-fourth; increasing the distance threefold reduces his exposure to one-ninth. Remote handling devices use this principle to reduce exposure.

(c) Shielding. Shielding materials absorb a part or all of the energy of the various types of radiation. Interposing a shield between the individual and the radiation source reduces the amount of radiation exposure.

(d) Radioactive Decay. All radioactive materials decay exponentially at a fixed time rate. The time required for a radioactive substance to decrease to one-half its original activity is called the half-life of that particular substance. Thus, allowing the radioactive material to decay for a period of time will reduce the amount of exposure received when the material is handled.

Chapter 5
EXPOSURE RECORDS

5-1. Introduction

(1) All personnel monitoring for occupational exposure to ionizing radiation must be documented to establish individual radiation exposure histories. These histories have medical, epidemiological and legal significance since they record the amounts of exposure as well as dates and locations at which exposures were received. Additionally, they serve as evidence that occupational exposure limits were or were not exceeded. This chapter contains the recording and reporting procedures the Chief, Bureau of Medicine and Surgery considers necessary and adequate for radiation exposure documentation. Reporting requirements contained herein have been approved by the Chief of Naval Operations.

(2) Monitored exposure to ionizing radiation is normally recorded on NAVMED Form 6470/10, Record of Occupational Exposure to Ionizing Radiation and NAVMED Form 6470/11, Record of Occupational Exposure to Ionizing Radiation From Internally Deposited Radionuclides. The predecessor to these forms was the DD Form 1141. NAVMED Forms 6470/10 and 6470/11 and DD Form 1141 are to be filed and maintained in the health record and in no other location.

(3) For activities holding Radioactive Material Permits, the NAVMED Form 6470/10 and NAVMED Form 6470/11 shall be used in lieu of NRC Form 4, Occupational External Radiation History and NRC Form 5, Current Occupational External Radiation Exposure.

5-2. Computerized Exposure Record Systems

(1) Computerized exposure record systems are required. Request for exceptions to this requirement will be forwarded to BUMED (MED-21). The Naval Dosimetry Center will provide, upon request, a personal computer (PC) program for automation of exposure records and reports required by this manual. Locally prepared or other programs may be used if approved by Chief, BUMED. Locally prepared or other programs must be compatible with the databases used by the Naval Dosimetry Center if reports are to be transmitted on magnetic media. (The Shipyard ARCMIS and the Shipboard Non-tactical ADP Program (SNAP) Automated Medical System (SAMS), and the Radiation Health Assistant (RHA) supported by the Naval Dosimetry Center are approved programs.)

(a) Personnel exposure information will be entered in the computerized database at least once a quarter.

(b) The computer generated NAVMED Forms 6470/10 and 6470/11 printouts are to be filed at least annually in the individual's medical record.

(c) A back-up copy (separate disk or magnetic tape) of the exposure information database must be made at least quarterly and retained for two quarters.

(d) Requests for exceptions to the requirement to submit reports via magnetic media and maintain computerized exposure record systems will be forwarded to Chief, BUMED, explaining the reason submission needs to be on a manually prepared report.

5-3. Record of Occupational Exposure to Ionizing Radiation (NAVMED Form 6470/10)

(1) *General*. The custodian of the individual's health record shall prepare and maintain a NAVMED Form 6470/10, for each person monitored for exposure to ionizing radiation.

(2) *Initial Determination*. For the initial preparation of NAVMED Form 6470/10 reasonable effort should be made to obtain complete reports of all previous exposures based upon recorded personnel dosimetry. This shall be accomplished by correspondence with previous commands, employers and/or the Naval Dosimetry Center.

(a) For each period in which the individual was monitored for occupational exposure to ionizing radiation and no record or an incomplete record of the exposure during the period can be obtained, an entry will be made indicating exposure data was incomplete or not available. An estimate of prior Lifetime Total Effective Dose Equivalent may be made based on partial records, exposure of others performing similar work, and statements from the individual. If an estimate is made, the basis for the estimate will be explained in the remarks section.

(b) When an individual was previously exposed at more than one facility, the exposure from each facility shall be separately recorded in items 7 through 14, as appropriate.

(c) If an individual has been occupationally exposed at any activity possessing a Nuclear Regulatory Commission License, and his exposures have been recorded on NRC-4 and NRC-5 forms, the cumulative exposure obtained from those forms shall be recorded on the NAVMED Form 6470/10 in items 7 through 14, as appropriate, and a statement regarding the source of that information shall be entered in the remarks section of the NAVMED Form 6470/10.

(3) *Current Record*. Appropriate entries on each individual's NAVMED Form 6470/10 or an update of the individual's computerized exposure database which can generate this form shall be made at least quarterly for those personnel monitored for exposure.

(a) Entries on the NAVMED Form 6470/10 are to be completed per the guidance provided below and the instructions on the back of the form. The method of monitoring is presumed to be by TLD after 1 October 1989 and no entry explaining the type of dosimeter is required in the Remarks section unless the method of monitoring is not a TLD.

(b) All previous copies of NAVMED Form 6470/10 and DD Form 1141, Record of Occupational Exposure to Ionizing Radiation filed in the individual's medical record shall be retained in the individual's medical records.

(c) The instructions on the NAVMED Form 6470/10, items 7 and 8 require the entering of the period of exposure (beginning and end). Items 9 through 13, require the entering of the radiation dose received for the period of exposure. For calcium fluoride TLDs used by forces afloat, the period of exposure and the radiation dose for the period entered on the NAVMED Form 6470/10 shall be the same as the issue period (beginning and end) recorded in blocks 6/7 and 11 of the exposure record card (Subgen Form 9890/30). The radiation dose received for the period shall be the same as the cumulative total of radiation doses recorded in block 10 of the exposure record card. Multiple entries on the NAVMED Form 6470/10, to document periods of leave etc., which occur routinely during any given issue period/period of exposure are not necessary.

(d) Personnel exposure data shall be obtained and properly recorded on the NAVMED Form 6470/10. Entries should identify the dates of the exposure and either the installation where the individual is permanently assigned or if exposed while on temporary duty assignment, the activity where the exposure was received. Use of hull numbers for identification is considered appropriate for afloat commands.

(e) When an individual is monitored for exposure to ionizing radiation at a naval installation or activity, other than where his medical records are maintained, the commanding officer, or officer in charge of that installation or activity shall ensure the personnel exposure information is furnished to the custodian of the individual's medical record. This exposure information shall be forwarded to the health record custodian at least quarterly or within 30 days of receipt of final personnel exposure information. Exposures received by visiting or temporary duty personnel whose exposures are not reported annually by their parent activities, shall be submitted to the Naval Dosimetry Center, Navy Environmental Health Center Detachment, Bethesda, MD 20889-5614 on a Situational Report, NAVMED Form 6470/1 by the command where the exposure occurred.

(f) When an individual is monitored for exposure to ionizing radiation at an installation outside the jurisdiction of the Department of the Navy, the individual shall ensure the exposure data is furnished to the custodian of his medical record for entry on the NAVMED Form 6470/10, and submission on a NAVMED Form 6470/1, Annual or Situational Report.

(g) Annual verification of the Lifetime Total Effective Dose Equivalent (column 14 of the NAVMED Form 6470/10) is required if the entries are prepared manually. If the NAVMED Form 6470/10 is generated using an approved computer program, that has not been modified since approval, annual verification of the total effective dose equivalent is not required.

5-4. Record of Occupational Exposure to Ionizing Radiation from Internally Deposited Radionuclides (NAVMED Form 6470/11)

(1) Results of all internal monitoring including baseline measurements shall be recorded on a NAVMED Form 6470/11 and the results reported in the Committed Effective Dose Equivalent column of the NAVMED Forms 6470/10 and 6470/1, Annual or Situational Report of Exposure to Ionizing Radiation. Instructions are provided on the back of the forms.

(a) The results of internal monitoring shall include the following information: date of monitoring, the system's minimum detectable activity (MDA), the isotope(s) for which monitoring was performed, activity (in units of nanocuries) present and the anatomical locations monitored. Additionally, the equipment type and serial number will be recorded in those cases where an individual has been exposed to airborne radioactivity above the limits of the applicable program radiological controls manual, or greater than minimum detectable activity (MDA) is identified during internal monitoring. If a series of monitoring measurements are performed within one week following an occupational exposure which resulted in internal contamination, then the time as well as the date of each monitoring shall also be recorded. In this case, the committed effective dose equivalent is calculated based on intake and retention determined from the series of measurements, and a single entry is made in column 12 of the NAVMED Form 6470/11 for the series of measurements. Only one committed effective dose equivalent entry will be made per internal contamination. If nonnaturally occurring, or abnormal amounts of radioisotopes not related to an occupational exposure are detected, e.g., isotopes administered for medical purposes, cesium-137 from consuming venison, etc., the detection shall be noted in the remarks section of the NAVMED Form 6470/11.

(b) If internal monitoring is performed on an individual during an issue period where the individual is monitored for deep dose (photon or neutron) the committed effective dose equivalent entry in column 12 of the NAVMED Form 6470/11 will be transcribed to column 12 of the NAVMED Form 6470/10 for that issue period. For example, if the external monitoring period is 1 February 1992 to 28 February 1992 and the internal monitoring is performed on 5 February 1992 then a committed effective dose equivalent entry would be made for the 1 February 1992 to 28 February 1992 monitoring period. If internal monitoring is completed and the individual is not being monitored for deep dose then the committed effective dose entry on the NAVMED Form 6470/11 will be transcribed to the NAVMED Form 6470/10 and the issue period ("From" and "To") will be the date the internal monitoring was performed.

(2) Results of internal monitoring measurements which show internal contamination from occupational exposure greater than the MDA of the counting equipment shall be forwarded to the Naval Dosimetry Center or authorized facility for calculation of the committed effective dose equivalent. The results will be returned to the submitting activity for incorporation on the NAVMED Forms 6470/10, 6470/11 and 6470/1.

(a) Local activities may calculate the committed effective dose equivalent if specifically authorized by Chief, BUMED. Activities requesting authorization must submit their procedures to Chief, BUMED for review and approval. However, all calculated committed effective dose equivalent shall be reviewed by Chief, BUMED (MED-21) prior to entry into an individual's exposure record.

(b) Naval shipyards are authorized to calculate the committed effective dose equivalent.

(c) The committed effective dose equivalent is calculated by:

(1) Following the methodology recommended by the International Commission on Radiological Protection (ICRP) in ICRP Report Number 30. Calculations should be based on activity measurements determined at least 24 hours after the exposure event. Total exposure may be based on the retention rates in ICRP 30 or on measured retention rates as observed for the exposed individual, or;

(2) Comparing the measured air concentration values and exposure time with the DAC limits (40 hours per week, 50 weeks per year exposure to yield 5 rem (0.05 Sv)) and calculating the committed effective dose equivalent.

(3) Internal monitoring measurements which are less than the minimum detectable activity (MDA) of the counting equipment shall be recorded on the NAVMED Form 6470/11 as less than MDA (<MDA) and the committed effective dose equivalent will be entered as 00.000 rem.

(4) For internal monitoring of organs where the organ dose limit is more limiting than the committed effective dose equivalent, e.g., thyroid monitoring for iodine uptake, a separate NAVMED Form 6470/11 will be maintained. At the top and bottom of the form the name of the organ should be written. For example, for thyroid monitoring the words "Thyroid Monitoring" will be written or typed at the top and bottom of the form. The word "Effective" in the heading for column 12 will be lined out so the heading reads "Committed Dose Equivalent." Internal monitoring measurements which are less than the MDA of the counting equipment shall be recorded on the NAVMED Form 6470/11 as less than MDA (<MDA) and the committed dose equivalent entered as 00.000 rem. Results of internal monitoring measurements greater than the MDA of the counting equipment for the isotope(s) of concern shall be forwarded to the Naval Dosimetry Center or authorized facility (see Article 5-4(2)) for calculation of the organ committed dose equivalent. To determine compliance with the organ dose limits of Chapter 4, the deep dose equivalent from external exposure must be added to the committed dose equivalent. The committed dose equivalent is multiplied by the organ weighting factor to give the committed effective dose equivalent.

5-5. Cross Checks and Verification

(1) To ensure accurate transcription and recording of dosimetry information a random sampling of the exposure data in the data-base, or on printed computer formatted NAVMED Forms 6470/10 and 6470/11, or on manually prepared NAVMED Forms 6470/10 and 6470/11 shall be cross checked against appropriate records, e.g., exposure record cards, NAVMED Form 6470/3, Radiation Exposure Reports, or comparable records. This cross check shall be performed semiannually on 1 percent of the individual records in the computerized database or no less than five of the individual records. If errors are found, a larger percentage of the records should be checked. The cross check shall be noted by making an entry in the remarks section of the database for the audited NAVMED Forms 6470/10 and 6470/11 or by signing and dating a statement in the remarks section of the printed NAVMED Forms 6470/10 and 6470/11 that entries have been verified.

(1) Manually prepared NAVMED Forms 6470/10 and 6470/11 shall be individually verified on an annual basis normally in conjunction with preparation of the annual report. This verification will consist of an audit of the past year's exposure entries to verify correct addition. If the NAVMED Forms 6470/10 and 6470/11 are generated using an approved computer program that has not been modified since approval, annual verification is not required.

(3) If erroneous entries have been made on manually prepared NAVMED Forms 6470/10 or 6470/11, they shall not be stricken out. A new entry which corrects the error(s) shall

be made. An explanation of the error and the correction shall be briefly documented by a dated entry in the remarks section. An asterisk (*) or footnote number shall be neatly entered in the block containing the erroneous entry. This procedure for correcting erroneous entries on the NAVMED Forms 6470/10 and 6470/11 supersedes the requirements of Chapter 16 of the Manual of the Medical Department for correction of medical record entries.

5-6. Dose Investigations and Dose Estimates

(1) When a primary dosimetric device, (e.g., a thermoluminescent dosimeter) is lost, damaged, or destroyed, the medical officer, radiation health officer, or medical department representative, as applicable, shall be notified and doses shall be estimated based on:

(a) Exposure time and radiation levels;

(b) Dose of other personnel performing similar work, or the individual's previously recorded dose while performing similar work;

(c) Pocket dosimeter measurements, if available.

All of the above procedures for estimating dose shall be used and recorded in an investigation report, contingent on the availability of data. The investigation report shall include a description of how the dosimetric device was lost, damaged, or destroyed, the dose estimate, the period covered by the estimate, work performed by the individual during this period, a description of the investigation, results from each estimating procedure, and applicable supporting documentation (e.g., any calculations performed, copies of radiation survey records, or copies of abnormal thermoluminescent dosimeter glow curves). The dose assigned, based on the investigation, shall be the "best estimate" of the dose received as opposed to "worst case" or "most conservative" estimate. The investigation report shall be approved in writing by the medical officer or the radiation health officer. For commands not having a medical officer or a radiation health officer, the investigation report should be approved by the medical department representative and the executive officer. The investigation report shall not be entered in the individual's health record. The investigation report shall be retained indefinitely.

(1) A dose estimate shall also be performed when the results of the primary dosimetric device are considered suspect. If the investigation concludes the results are not suspect, an estimate is not required. For example a dose estimate shall be performed when:

(a) An abnormal glow curve is observed for a thermoluminescent dosimeter.

(b) The measurement of gamma or x-ray radiation by the whole body primary dosimetric device, e.g., a thermoluminescent dosimeter, differs significantly from the measurement by the whole body secondary dosimetric device, e.g., a pocket dosimeter, and both devices have been worn together at the same body location. Examples of "significant differences" are provided below.

(1) Primary and secondary dosimetric device measurements differ by 30 percent or more and the primary dosimetric device measurement is greater than or equal to 100 mrem.

(2) Primary and secondary dosimetric device measurements differ by 30 mrem or more and the primary dosimetric device measurement is less than 100 mrem.

(3) Primary and secondary dosimetric device measurements differ by 100 mrem or more and the secondary device is an intermediate range pocket dosimeter (IM-181/PD).

(4) Primary and secondary dosimetric device measurements differ by 300 mrem or more and the secondary device is a high range pocket dosimeter (IM-135/PD).

(5) Primary and secondary dosimetric device differ by more than the criteria established in the applicable technical manual for nonstandard secondary dosimetric devices, e.g., RADSTAR or other electronic dosimeters.

(c) The measurement of neutron radiation by the primary dosimetric device differs significantly from the expected dose. Examples of "significant difference" are provided below:

(1) Primary and expected doses differ by 100 percent or more and the primary dosimetric device measurement is greater than or equal to 30 mrem of neutron dose.

(2) Primary and expected doses differ by 30 mrem or more and the primary dosimetric device measurement is less than 30 mrem of neutron dose.

(3) The reason why the dose estimate was performed, the dose estimate, the basis for the dose estimate, and the period covered by the estimate shall be recorded in the "Remarks" section of the NAVMED Form 6470/10 or on an addendum to the NAVMED Form 6470/10. A description of how the dosimetry device was lost, damaged, or destroyed shall not be recorded on the NAVMED Form 6470/10 or on an addendum to NAVMED Form 6470/10. The entry must be concise and will normally be limited to a few summary statements. If the entry is made on an addendum to NAVMED Form 6470/10, the entry shall not exceed one page in length. Summary statements of less than 600 spaces concerning a dose estimate shall be transcribed to the NAVMED Form 6470/1 upon submission of the annual or situational report of personnel exposure to ionizing radiation or as a footnote if submitted in computer format.

5-7. External Contamination

(1) Results of all cases of external personnel contamination shall be recorded in the remarks section of the individual's NAVMED Form 6470/10, Record of Exposure to Ionizing Radiation, and reported in the remarks section of a situational report or on the annual report, NAVMED Form 6470/1.

(a) The results shall include the following minimum information: date of monitoring, isotope(s) monitored, activity (in units of microcuries or nanocuries) present, and the anatomical location of the contamination.

(b) A form covering this information may be marked as "Addendum to NAVMED 6470/10" and incorporated with the NAVMED Form 6470/10 in the health record.

5-8. Extremity Exposure

(1) For individuals who are monitored for exposure to the extremities, as defined in Chapter 1, a separate NAVMED Form 6470/10 for extremity exposure shall be maintained. The words "Extremity Monitoring" will be written or typed at the top and bottom of the NAVMED Form 6470/10. The highest measured exposure will be recorded as the extremity exposure when multiple extremities are monitored. Extremity exposures will be recorded in column 9, Shallow Dose. Columns 10 through 14 will be left blank. Do not transfer this entry to column 9 of the whole body NAVMED Form 6470/10. Extremity shallow dose equivalent shall be maintained separately, and shall be reported to the Naval Dosimetry Center in either the remarks section or on a separate page or pages of the annual or situational report of personnel exposure to ionizing radiation, NAVMED Form 6470/1. The reported doses shall be clearly annotated as extremity doses.

5-9. Eye Exposure

(1) For individuals who are monitored for exposure to the eyes, a separate NAVMED Form 6470/10 for eye exposure shall be maintained. The words "Eye Monitoring" will be written or typed at the top and bottom of the NAVMED Form 6470/10. The word "Shallow" in column 9 will be lined out and replaced with the word "Eye." Eye exposures will be recorded in column 9. Columns 10 through 14 will be left blank.

5-10. Embryo/Fetus Exposure

(1) In order for the embryo/fetus exposure limits of Chapter 4 to apply a woman monitored for radiation exposure must inform her command, in writing, of her pregnancy. To ensure its documentation and retention, the written declaration shall be made on a Standard Form 600, Chronological Record of Medical Care (SF-600), and placed in the woman's health record. The following SF-600 entry shall be completed, dated and signed by the woman and witnessed by a representative of the medical department:

"I hereby make notification I am pregnant. My estimated date of conception is _____. I understand by declaring my pregnancy, my occupational exposure to ionizing radiation will be controlled so that the dose to my unborn child does not exceed the limits prescribed in Chapter 4 of NAVMED P-5055, the Navy Radiation Health Protection Manual."

(2) When the woman declares her pregnancy the exposure to the embryo/fetus from the estimated date of conception will be calculated. Future exposure to the woman will be carefully monitored to ensure the exposure limits in Chapter 4 for the embryo/fetus are not exceeded. When the exposure to the embryo/fetus ends, either by termination of pregnancy or termination of employment of the declared pregnant woman, the Total Effective Dose Equivalent to the embryo/fetus shall be calculated based on the conception date and entered in the Remarks section of the woman's NAVMED From 6470/10.

(3) At the conclusion of her pregnancy, the woman must notify her command of the date the pregnancy ended so that the Total Effective Dose Equivalent to the embryo/fetus can be calculated and her exposure limit can be modified back to her whole body limit. An entry shall be made on a Standard Form 600 (SF-600) and placed in the woman's health record documenting the date the declared pregnancy ended.

5-11. Termination Letters

(1) If radiation workers are released, retired or terminate employment and request a copy of their exposure information, they shall be provided with a statement of their total occupational radiation exposure received during their period of employment or service with the Navy or Marine Corps. The termination letter shall be submitted within 30 days of the receipt of the individual's final exposure information or final determination the individual will no longer be monitored for exposure to ionizing radiation. The termination letter shall include:

(a) Name, social security number, and date of birth of the individual.

(b) Exposure Information. Exposure information from all NAVMED Form 6470/10s and DD Form 1141s shall be extracted and summarized for all categories of monitored exposure. The current year's exposure shall be listed by quarter year. For prior years the exposures shall be listed by command and location or hull number, period monitored at that command, and cumulative Navy exposure during that time period. The period monitored shall be in day, month, year format from the date first monitored to the date last monitored at the command, inclusive. Exposures received prior to January 1992 may be listed as whole body exposures with internal monitoring listed separately as listed on the DD Form 1141 or may be converted to effective dose equivalents. To convert prior DD Form 1141 exposures to shallow dose equivalent, shallow dose equivalent to the extremities, eye dose, deep dose equivalent, total effective dose equivalent and lifetime total effective dose equivalent:

(1) Shallow Dose Equivalent. If monitored for skin exposure, shallow dose will be entered as equal to the numeric value of the skin dose (column 9), of the DD Form 1141 for the periods monitored. If not monitored, leave this column blank.

(2) Deep dose equivalent, photon will be entered as equal to the value of the

gamma and x-ray dose (column 10) of DD Form 1141.

(3) Deep dose equivalent, neutron will be entered as equal to the value of the neutron dose (column 11) of the DD Form 1141.

(4) Committed Effective Dose Equivalent. If internal monitoring was conducted and the results indicated a positive uptake the committed effective dose equivalent shall be calculated by a BUMED approved facility (see Article 5-4(2)) using the ICRP methodology. Internal monitoring results less than the system's MDA shall be recorded as 00.000 rem committed effective dose equivalent. If no internal monitoring was performed, leave this column blank.

(5) Total effective dose equivalent will be entered as the sum of deep dose equivalent, photon, deep dose equivalent, neutron and committed effective dose equivalent.

(c) The following statements shall be included on the form or letter provided to the individual:

(1) "This report is per NAVMED P-5055, Radiation Health Protection Manual."

(2) "You should preserve this report for future reference. If you should seek future employment involving occupational exposure to ionizing radiation, your employer will want this information. As a point of reference to the significance of your exposure, the average exposure to a member of the United States population is approximately 300 mrem (3 mSv) per year from natural background radiation. Federal radiation exposure limits are 5 rem (0.05 Sv) per year, total effective dose equivalent. No adverse observable effect is expected at exposure levels below the Federal limits."

5-12. Required Reports

(1) *Annual Report of Personnel Exposure to Ionizing Radiation to the Individual.* Annually, any installation, activity, ship or unit at which personnel are monitored for exposure to ionizing radiation, shall provide all monitored individuals currently onboard a written report of their dose for the previous calendar year. This annual report shall be provided prior to 1 April each year. If valid operational commitments (e.g., SSBN patrol cycle) delay receipt of final personnel exposure information for the previous year until after 1 March, the report shall be provided within 30 days of the date of receipt of final personnel exposure information.

(2) *Annual Reports of Personnel Exposure to Ionizing Radiation.*

(a) Annually, any installation, activity, ship or unit at which personnel are monitored for exposure to sources of ionizing radiation, shall submit an annual report of personnel exposure to ionizing radiation on NAVMED Form 6470/1, report of personnel exposure to ionizing radiation, in magnetic media format to the Naval Dosimetry Center. Acceptable submission will be on 3.5 inch diskettes and will include a printed copy of

the tabulated report. This annual report shall be submitted prior to 1 April each year. If valid operational commitments (e.g., SSBN patrol cycle) delay receipt of final exposure information for the previous year until after 1 March, the annual report shall be submitted within 30 days of the date of receipt of final personnel exposure information. These reports shall be submitted to:

Officer in Charge
Naval Dosimetry Center
Navy Environmental Health Center
  Detachment
Bethesda, MD 20889-5614

(b) This report shall include those personnel on board 31 December who have been monitored for exposure to ionizing radiation during the previous calendar year while assigned to the reporting activity. Dosimetry readings of 00.000 rem are required to be reported. If the individual was not monitored for a given type of radiation or if the individual did not receive monitoring for internal contamination leave the appropriate column(s) blank.

(c) For badging periods that span 1 January, the year in which the mid-point of the exposure period occurs shall be the year in which the entire exposure for that period is reported.

(3) *Situational Report of Personnel Exposure to Ionizing Radiation.*

(a) If a monitored individual is transferred, retires or terminates employment, prior to 31 December, a Situational Report of Personnel Exposure to Ionizing Radiation shall be submitted on NAVMED Form 6470/1 in magnetic media format by the individual's activity to the Naval Dosimetry Center within 30 days of detachment of the individual from the command, or within 30 days of receipt of the individual's final exposure information, whichever is later. Acceptable submission will be on 3.5 inch diskettes and will include a printed copy of the tabulated report.

(b) If a visitor at a naval facility or an individual on temporary duty from an activity which does not submit annual or situational reports of personnel exposure to ionizing radiation, is monitored for exposure to ionizing radiation, a situational report of personnel exposure to ionizing radiation, submitted in magnetic media format, shall be prepared and forwarded to the Naval Dosimetry Center by the activity at which the exposure was incurred, within 30 days of departure of the individual from the command or receipt of the individual's exposure information.

(c) The exposure reported on a situational report of personnel exposure to ionizing radiation for an individual terminating or transferring shall be only that exposure for the year in which transfer or termination occurs. Do not summarize the individual's complete exposure history on a situational report.

(4) *Situational Report of Personnel Exceeding Radiation Exposure Limits.* This report shall be submitted to Chief, BUMED, Attention: Undersea Medicine and Radiation Health Division, as follows:

(a) If any individual (adult radiation worker, nonradiation worker, minor, declared pregnant woman, or member of the general public) receives a total effective dose equivalent in excess of the limits specified in Chapter 4, this report shall be forwarded on NAVMED Form 6470/1 within 30 days from the determination of such exposure. Details explaining how the exposure was received will be entered in the remarks section of the form or as an attachment to the report. The report may be submitted in a manual format. The report shall include:

(1) The individual's dose; and,

(2) The levels of radiation and concentrations of radioactive material involved; and,

(3) The cause of the elevated exposures, dose rates, or concentrations; and,

(4) The corrective actions taken or planned to ensure against a recurrence.

(b) If any individual receives a total effective dose equivalent of more than 5 rem (0.05 Sv), eye dose equivalent exceeding 15 rem (0.15 Sv), or a shallow dose equivalent of 50 rem (0.5 Sv) in a single incident, BUMED, Undersea Medicine and Radiation Health Division, shall be notified immediately by telephone and/or "IMMEDIATE" message. During "MINIMIZE," electrical transmission by priority message is authorized. A follow-up written report shall be forwarded on NAVMED Form 6470/1 within 24 hours from the determination of such exposure. The Report may be submitted in a manual format.

(c) If an individual receives a total effective dose equivalent of more than 25 rem (0.25 Sv) or an eye dose equivalent of 75 rem (0.75 Sv), or a shallow dose equivalent of 250 rad (2.5 Gy) in a single event, BUMED, Undersea Medicine and Radiation Health Division, shall be notified immediately by telephone and/or "IMMEDIATE" message. During "MINIMIZE," electrical transmission by priority message is authorized. A detailed Situational Report of Personnel Exceeding Radiation Exposure Limits furnishing all information available on the exposure, the reason for such exposure, the general status of health and physical condition of the individual and a summary of treatment rendered or recommended, shall be submitted to BUMED, Undersea Medicine and Radiation Health Division, at the earliest practicable time following the exposure. In any event, this amplifying report must be submitted within 15 days after exposure. A copy of this report shall be placed in the individual's health record as an addendum to the NAVMED Form 6470/10.

(5) *Instructions for Completion of NAVMED Form 6470/1, Radiation Exposure Report in Computer Format.* Data will be prepared according to the following specifications and format:

(a) Three and a half inch (720 kilobytes or 1.44 megabyte) diskettes used for submission shall be in PC format. The diskette label shall include the following information:

1) ANNUAL REPORT OF PERSONNEL EXPOSURE TO IONIZING RADIATION or SITUATIONAL REPORT OF PERSONNEL EXPOSURE TO IONIZING RADIATION

(2) Name of Command, UIC

(3) Command Point of Contact

(4) Telephone Number if appropriate.

(b) Data submitted on magnetic media will be formatted in records of 113 character length. Each record is terminated with a carriage return and line feed. The data will be arranged in each record according to the format listed below:

Field

1   Character columns 1 through 4 shall be blank.

2   Unit Identification Code: Enter the 5 digit unit identification code of the reporting command in columns 5 through 9.

3   Name: Enter the name as last name, first name and middle initial placing 1 space between each and omitting any punctuation marks, in columns 10 through 49. If necessary, limit the name to 40 columns by truncation.

4   Social Security Number: Enter each individual's 9 digit SSN, without hyphens, in columns 50 through 58. For personnel not possessing a United States Social Security Number, enter a pseudo SSN as: 800 for the first three digits, the year, month, and day of birth (i.e., 800-YY-MMDD).

5   Date of Birth: Enter the individual's 4-digit year of birth in columns 59 through 62. Enter the month of birth in columns 63 and 64. Use a leading zero in any single digit entry, e.g., June 1956 would be entered as 195606.

6   Occupational Code: Where applicable, enter the 2-digit occupational code as described on the reverse side of NAVMED Form 6470/1 in columns 65 and 66. Individuals receiving exposure from more than one program should be assigned the occupational code which represents their primary source of exposure.

10: Nuclear Propulsion (Radiation Worker)
11: Nuclear Propulsion (Non-radiation Worker.)

12: Nuclear Propulsion (Visitor, not included in other Nuclear Propulsion Programs)
20: Nuclear Weapons (Radiation Worker)
21: Nuclear Weapons (Non-radiation Worker)
22: Nuclear Weapons (Visitor)
30: Diagnostic Radiology
31: Dental
32: Nuclear Medicine
33: Radiation Oncology
40: Gamma Radiography
41: X-ray Radiography and Accelerators of energies less than 10 MeV
42: Accelerators of energies greater than 10 MeV
43: RADIAC Calibration
44: General Industrial sources (moisture density meters, analytical x-ray sources, depleted uranium, electron microscopes, etc.)
50: Research
51: Research (Radioisotope)
90: Other

7   Exposure Date: Enter the year, month, and day, on which exposure began as follows: 4 digit year in columns 67 through 70, month in columns 71 and 72, and day in columns 73 and 74, using a leading zero in any month or day entry that is only a single digit. In the same order and manner, enter the year, month, and day exposure ended in columns 75 through 82.

8   Shallow Dose Equivalent: Enter the individual's shallow dose equivalent in mrem in columns 83 through 87. This entry is skin shallow dose equivalent. Do not report extremity shallow dose equivalent in this field. A 5 digit format, excluding any decimal point will be used. Use leading zeros to fill the entire field. If not monitored, leave the field blank. Zero exposures must be recorded.

9   Deep Dose Equivalent, Photon: Enter the individual's deep dose equivalent, photon using the above described dose format, in columns 88 through 92. If not monitored, leave the field blank. Zero exposures must be recorded.

10   Deep Dose Equivalent, Neutron: Enter the individual's deep dose equivalent, neutron using the above described dose format, in columns 93 through 97. If not monitored leave the field blank. Zero exposures must be recorded.

11   Committed Effective Dose Equivalent: Enter the individual's committed effective dose equivalent using the above described dose format, in columns 98 through 102. If not monitored, leave the field blank. Zero exposures must be recorded.

12   Total Effective Dose Equivalent This Period: Enter the total of field 9, (deep dose equivalent, photon), field 10 (deep dose equivalent, neutron) and field 11 (committed effective dose equivalent) using the above described dose format, in columns 103 through 107. If not applicable, leave the field blank. Zero exposure must be recorded.

13   Lifetime Total Effective Dose Equivalent: Enter the lifetime total effective dose equivalent of the individual as of the end of the reported period. A 6 digit format excluding any decimal point will be used. Leave the hundreds place blank for exposures less than 100.000 rem (1.0 Sv). Use the above described format in columns 108 through 113 .

(6) *Instructions for Completion of NAVMED Form 6470/1, Report of Personnel Exposure to Ionizing Radiation in Manual Format.*

(a) In the heading of the form, check the two appropriate boxes to indicate whether the report is an annual report or a situational report and, whether it is a report of personnel exposure to ionizing radiation, or a report of personnel exceeding radiation exposure limits.

(b) Items 1 through 17.

1   Enter name and address of reporting activity.

2   Enter UIC. Enter the 5 digit Unit Identification Code of the reporting command. It is extremely important the UIC be correct. The Naval Radiation Exposure Registry is a UIC based database.

3   Enter calendar year reported.

4   Enter date prepared.

5   Enter name as currently carried on rolls last name, first and middle initial, as appropriate. If necessary, limit the name to 40 columns by truncation.

6   Enter individual's SSN. For personnel not possessing a United States Social Security Number, enter a pseudo SSN as: 800 for the first three digits, the year, month, and day of birth (i.e., 800-YY-MMDD).

7   Enter individual's year and month of birth. Enter the year as 4 digits and the month as 2 digits. For the month of birth use the appropriate

digits from 01 for January through 12 for December. For example, an individual born in April 1980 would have the entry 198004.

8   Enter the individual's occupational code in which the majority of exposure occurred.

9   Enter year, month, and day exposure was considered to have started since last report, i.e, 19990101.

10   Enter year, month and day exposure was considered to have ended, i.e. 19991231.

11-16   Enter radiation dose equivalents received to three decimal places, i.e., 03.450. Enter dose equivalents evaluated as "zero" as 00.000. Do not use "Xs" or term "minimal." If the individual was not monitored for a specific type of radiation exposure (e.g., neutron), leave the field blank.

11   Enter skin shallow dose equivalent in rem. Do not report extremity shallow dose equivalent in this field. Report extremity shallow dose equivalent in the remarks section, block 17, or on a separate page of the 6470/1. Clearly annotate as extremity dose.

12   Enter deep dose equivalent, photon, in rem.

13   Enter deep dose equivalent, neutron in rem.

14   Enter committed effective dose equivalent in rem.

15   Enter total effective dose equivalent for this period; sum of items 12, 13 and 14. This entry should normally be only for the current calendar year. Previous year's exposure should have already been reported on prior annual reports.

16   Enter total lifetime dose equivalent in rem, enter to 6 digits only if exposure is greater than 99.999 rem.

17, 18, 19   Selfexplanatory.

(7) *Naval Exposure Registry Summary Report*. By the end of the second quarter of each year the Naval Dosimetry Center shall prepare a summary report of the exposures received from Navy and Marine Corps sources and forward the report to Chief, BUMED. The report shall include the total person-rem, exposure profiles in 100 mrem increments (number of people exposed per exposure increment), and an exposure trend analysis for Navy as a whole and by occupational code. The report shall also include the total number of people exposed, the total number of activities reporting exposure and a narrative summary of any exposures exceeding the exposure limits.

5-13. Retention, Disposition and Release of Information

(1) The DD Form 1141 and NAVMED Forms 6470/10 and 6470/11 are permanent components of the individual's health record and should be safeguarded as such; however, commanding officers, authorized inspecting officials, and supervisors of persons occupationally exposed to ionizing radiation or the individual concerned may review the DD Form 1141s and NAVMED Forms 6470/10 and 6470/11 with the medical records custodian upon request. The medical records custodian may exchange exposure data with installations outside the jurisdiction of the Department of the Navy for any persons occupationally exposed at the installation upon written request, provided a release authorization signed by the exposed individual is forwarded with the request.

(2) When a civilian employee is not included in a Federal civilian employee health care service, DD Form 1141 and NAVMED Forms 6470/10 and 6470/11 shall be maintained as a permanent document in the employee's official personnel folder.

(3) All available dosimetry results shall be entered on NAVMED Forms 6470/10 and 6470/11 as appropriate prior to transfer of military personnel. Dosimetry results not recorded as of the date of transfer shall be forwarded to the individual's next duty station within 30 days of receipt of final personnel exposure information.

(4) The DD Form 1141, and NAVMED Forms 6470/10 and 6470/11 shall be permanently retained in the retired medical records of a service member who has been monitored for exposure to ionizing radiation during his service. When a member is released from active duty or retires prior to his/her exposure information being entered in his/her health record, a dose transmittal with instructions to enter the information in the medical record shall be forwarded for incorporation in the member's health record. For Navy and Marine Corps personnel, the dose transmittal should be forwarded to:

Department of Veterans Affairs
VARMC
P.O. Box 5020
St. Louis, MO 63115-8950
Tel: 1-800-827-1000/314-538-4500

(5) Copies of completed NAVMED Form 6470/1, Situational and Annual Reports of Personnel Exposure to Ionizing Radiation shall be retained indefinitely.

(6) Exposure investigation reports shall be retained indefinitely.

(7) Copies of Termination Letters shall be retained for 5 years.

(8) Copies of NAVMED Form 6470/3 shall be retained for 5 years.

(9) Retain and dispose of other radiation health program documents per SECNAV Instruction 5212.5 series and applicable program radiological controls manuals.

5-14. Working Copy of NAVMED Form 6470/1.

(1) To maintain accurate NAVMED Form 6470/10s and to submit accurate NAVMED Form 6470/1s, a reliable record system is essential. It is suggested each activity's record system contain a working copy of NAVMED Form 6470/1 on which is transcribed all required data from DD Form 1141 or NAVMED Form 6470/10 on any persons transferred, terminated or retired during the month. Computer generated records are satisfactory provided either the source documents or a back-up copy exists. This data shall be updated when the personnel dosimetry is processed and used to prepare the situational report. The working copy of the NAVMED Form 6470/1 should be destroyed when the required situational report is submitted.

5-15. Control of Radiation Exposure Information for Nuclear Powered Warships and Operational Prototypes

(1) Selected forms and reports containing aggregated (more than one individual) radiation exposure for crews of nuclear powered warships or operational prototypes generated on or after 01 January 1999 must be marked as NOFORN and handled as unclassified naval nuclear propulsion information per NAVSEA Instruction C5511.32 series. Reports included under this requirement are the situational report (Form 6470/1), annual report (Form 6470/1), and radiation exposure report (Form 6470/3) when completed with exposure information.

(a) For SSN/SSBN platforms, all forms and reports containing aggregated radiation exposure information shall be handled as unclassified NNPI.

(b) For CVN platforms only, reports containing aggregated radiation exposure information for crewmembers involved in propulsion plant operations shall be handled as unclassified NNPI. Forms and reports for crewmembers not involved in propulsion plant operations (e.g., medical and radiography personnel) remain unclassified and are not to be controlled as NOFORN. Splitting reports to create separate NOFORN and uncontrolled documents is not required or desired.

(2) Applicable forms and reports, including disk labels when forwarding electronic copies, shall be marked and handled per NAVSEA Instruction C5511.32 series.

(3) Corrective action to mark hard copies of forms and reports accumulated prior to 01 January 1999 is not required. However, this material should be otherwise safeguarded as NOFORN per NAVSEA Instruction C5511.32 series.

(4) Forms and reports for specific individuals only (6470/10 and 6470/11 forms in medical records and termination letters to individuals), reports from non-nuclear powered ships (including tenders), non-ship and non-prototype activities (e.g., shipyards and IMAs), and reports that provide a compilation of exposure data without ship-specific identifiers, remain unclassified and are not to be controlled as NOFORN.

Chapter 6
PERSONNEL DOSIMETRY

6-1. Introduction

(1) Personnel dosimetry is a technique for detecting and measuring an individual's exposure to ionizing radiation. The Bureau of Medicine and Surgery requires naval activities to maintain a dosimetry program for personnel who receive occupational exposure to ionizing radiation. Personnel dosimetry is used to measure an individual's radiation exposure and to aid in minimizing exposure. Personnel dosimetry has medical, epidemiological and legal significance and must be conscientiously practiced by trained personnel under competent supervision.

6-2. Monitoring

(1) Environmental Monitoring. Environmental monitoring shall be performed in areas accessible to the general public to verify members of the general public are not likely to exceed a total effective dose equivalent of 100 mrem (1 mSv) per year and the dose in any unrestricted area from external sources does not exceed 2 mrem (0.02 mSv) in one hour.

(2) Area Monitoring. Area monitoring shall be performed in areas accessible to non-radiation workers to ensure nonradiation workers do not exceed 500 mrem (5 mSv) per year considering occupancy factors and source usage.

(3) Personnel Monitoring. Personnel monitoring devices shall be worn by:

(a) All adult personnel who could potentially receive from sources external to the body a dose in excess of:

Total Effective Dose Equivalent
(Whole Body).................... 00.500 rem/yr
Shallow Dose Equivalent
(Extremities)................... 05.000 rem/yr
Shallow Dose Equivalent
(Skin)........................ 05.000 rem/yr
Eye Dose Equivalent
(Eyes)........................01.500 rem/yr

Sum of deep dose equivalent
and committed dose equivalent
for any organ or tissue other
than the lens of the eye
(organ dose)...................05.000 rem/yr

If the dose to the eye is expected to be less than or approximately equal to the deep dose equivalent, then whole body monitoring may be used in lieu of a special device for monitoring the eye dose. For example, in fluoroscopy a deep dose monitoring device worn at the collar to control deep dose body exposure will suffice to control the eye exposure.

(b) All personnel entering a high radiation area (i.e., an area where the exposure rate is greater than 100 mrem (1 mSv) per hour).

(c) Declared pregnant women who could potentially receive, from sources external to the body, a dose in excess of 50 mrem (0.5 mSv) to the embryo/fetus during the entire pregnancy.

(d) Minors who could potentially receive in 1 year from sources external to the body a dose in excess of 50 mrem (0.5 mSv).

(e) Radiographers and radiographers' assistants as defined in Title 10, Part 34 of the Code of Federal Regulations in addition to a self indicating and alarming dosimeter.

(f) Any other personnel deemed necessary.

(4) Internal Monitoring. Internal monitoring shall be performed on the following personnel:

(a) Adults whose duties are expected to exceed 10 percent of an ALI.

(b) Minors whose duties are expected to exceed a committed effective dose equivalent of 50 mrem (0.5 mSv) in 1 year.

(c) Declared pregnant women whose duties are expected to exceed a dose of 50 mrem (0.5 mSv) to the embryo/fetus from sources internal to the body during the course of the pregnancy.

6-3. Dosimetric Devices

(1) The type of dosimetric device or devices used to measure personnel exposure shall be specified by the commanding officer and approved by Chief, BUMED. Unless other types of dosimetry are approved by Chief, BUMED, the dosimetry program shall be based on dosimetry as described in this Chapter, and its use shall be under the cognizance of the designated radiation health/safety officer or senior medical representative present if no radiation health/safety officer is designated. Acceptable dosimetric devices include: (1) personnel dosimeters, DT-526 or DT-648; (2) wrist badges, DT-526 or DT-648; (3) EXT RAD-100 finger ring dosimeter; single LiF chips; (4) pocket dosimeters, IM Series/PD; electronic dosimeter; (5) environmental and area monitoring dosimeters, DT-526, DT-648, DT-648 TLD cards in a BUMED

Area Monitor (BAM); (6) accident dosimeters, DT-518, DT-526, DT-648; and (7) battlefield dosimeters, DT-60 or DT-236. Organizations associated with the Naval Nuclear Propulsion Program will perform dosimetry following the appropriate NAVSEA Radiological Controls Manual.

(2) *Personnel Dosimeters*. Personnel dosimeters are used to monitor deep and shallow dose. Personnel dosimeters are normally worn at the waist or chest. In unique situations where an individual is exposed in a high gradient field or an individual is expected to receive a partial body exposure, the monitoring device should be worn on or at the part of the body, e.g., head, neck, upper arm or thigh, expected to receive the highest exposure. Personnel dosimeters provide a very sensitive, accurate and dependable indication of the exposure to an individual. Because of their sensitivity, accuracy, and dependability, these are referred to as primary dosimetric devices. Lithium fluoride and calcium fluoride thermoluminescent materials are the sensitive elements of the two primary Navy personnel dosimeters, the DT-648 and DT-526 respectively. Thermoluminescent dosimetry is based on the measurement of radiation using a crystalline substance sensitive to radiation that, when heated, produces light output that is proportional to the amount of radiation exposure.

(3) *Wrist Badges and/or Finger Rings* are used to monitor extremities in special situations where a relatively high local exposure is expected. For certain special situations involving high level exposures, the wearing of wrist badges or finger rings containing thermoluminescent chips to measure radiation exposure to the extremities may be required.

(4) *Pocket Dosimeters/Electronic Dosimeters*. Pocket dosimeters are self indicating devices used to monitor exposure to gamma or x-ray radiation in situations where an immediate indication of the exposure is desirable. Pocket dosimeters are pencil shaped devices containing a small ionization chamber. These devices provide very sensitive and accurate indications of the exposure of the individual, however they are susceptible to shock, dirt, moisture and other environmental factors which may produce a false overresponse. Consequently, they are used as secondary dosimetry devices. An alternative to the pocket dosimeter is the electronic dosimeter which is normally battery powered, has a digital display of integrated dose and can be set to alarm at a preset dose or dose rate. Electronic dosimeters are used as secondary dosimetric devices.

(5) *Environmental and Area Monitoring Dosimeters*. Environmental and area monitoring dosimeters are used at the perimeter of radiation areas or in uncontrolled spaces in conjunction with occupancy factors to verify members of the general public and nonradiation workers are not exposed in excess of the limits established in Chapter 4. They should not be posted in known high radiation areas or any other restricted area. Specific program requirements are in program radiological controls manuals.

(6) *Accident Dosimeters*. Accident dosimeters are used to monitor areas or personnel in situations where very high exposure may occur as the result of an accident. These dosimeters are less accurate than personnel dosimeters but have a much higher range.

(7) Battlefield Dosimeters. Battlefield dosimeters are used to medically triage personnel to maximize viable personnel assets. These dosimeters are less accurate than personnel dosimeters but have a much higher range.

(8) *Special Purpose Dosimetry*. Special purpose dosimetry is used to measure the exposure from unique or special sources, e.g., low energy x-rays, high energy protons, high energy heavy particles, very low or high intensity sources, etc., or to measure special radiation fields in unique or special settings. Dosimetry for special or unique situations may be obtained from the Naval Dosimetry Center.

(9) For further information or clarification, technical or administrative, concerning naval personnel dosimetry contact the Naval Dosimetry Center by telephone, letter or message:

Officer in Charge
Naval Dosimetry Center
Navy Environmental Health Center Detachment
Bethesda, MD, 20889-5614

The Naval Dosimetry Center's Plain Language Address for message traffic is:

NAVENVIRHLTHCEN DET BETHESDA MD.

The telephone numbers are:
DSN: 295-0142/ 0403/ 6164
                Commercial:(301)295-0142/
                     0403/ 6164
TeleFax: (301)295-5981; DSN 295-5981

6-4. Lithium Fluoride (LiF) Thermoluminescent Dosimetry

(1) *General*. Thermoluminescent dosimetry is the measure of radiation using a crystalline substance sensitive to radiation, that when heated, produces light output that is proportional to the amount of radiation exposure. Ionizing radiation imparts energy to the substance that creates free electrons and hole pairs in impurities in the crystal structure. When the irradiated substance is heated in a controlled manner, the electrons deexcite and give off energy in the form of visible light. The total amount of light is proportional to the energy absorbed from the ionizing radiation.

(2) *Lithium Fluoride Dosimeters*. The lithium fluoride thermoluminescent dosimeter, referred to as the LiF TLD, is capable of detecting beta, gamma, x-ray, and neutron radiation. LiF is extremely sensitive to low level radiation exposure, including background radiation.

6-5. DT-648 Lithium Fluoride (LiF) Thermoluminescent Dosimetry Monitoring Program

(1) *General.* The DT-648 LiF TLD Dosimeter is designed to detect beta, gamma, x-ray and neutron radiation. This system has four LiF TLD chips on a card and is used with a black badge holder. The following paragraphs describe the use of the DT-648 for monitoring personnel and areas for ionizing radiation. The DT-648 is authorized for monitoring gamma, x-ray, beta, and neutron radiation. For neutron radiation monitoring with the DT-648, default energy correction factors provide a conservative dosimetry value and should normally be applied. For situations where refined dosimetry values are needed, specific neutron energy spectra correction factors can be obtained from the Naval Dosimetry Center.

(2) *Initiation.* To initiate personnel dosimetry services, submit a letter request to the Naval Dosimetry Center. The request should state the number of individuals to be monitored, the source(s) and type(s) of radiation to be monitored, the activity's unit identification code (UIC), a desired starting date for dosimetry services, a complete mailing address and name and telephone number of a point of contact. Activities shall send requests via their chain of command. Upon approval of the request, the Naval Dosimetry Center will forward a package containing the necessary equipment for initiating the program.

(3) *Implementation and Use.* Upon request by an activity and approval by the Naval Dosimetry Center, the following items will be sent to the activity.

(a) A set of TLDs-quantity determined per the activity's request;

(b) Twice the number of card holders as TLDs-one set to wear, and one set to work with when changing out the TLDs;

(c) Card holder openers;

(d) Optional identification and security stickers for the card holders;

(e) Optional card holder clips;

(f) A pad of report forms, "Radiation Exposure Report, NAVMED Form 6470/3";

(g) External warning labels for TLD card shipment containers;

(h) 3.5 inch floppy computer disk;

(i) A shipping list, and;

(j) The Radiation Health Assistant Program (RHA) on a set of computer disks.

(4) *The DT-648 Card.* The TLD card consists of four LiF:Mg, Ti TL elements of different thickness and composition mounted between two teflon sheets on an aluminum substrate. The TLD card holder covers each TL chip with a filter providing different radiation absorption thicknesses to allow evaluation of deep and shallow dose equivalents. Chips 1, 2 and 3 are Li-7, which is sensitive to photon and beta radiation. Chip 4 is Li-6, which is sensitive to photon, beta and neutron radiation. The card also has a bar code identification label across the face. This card, with four chips and bar code identification, shall be used only in the black card holder for personnel monitoring; no other holder is authorized. See Figure 1.

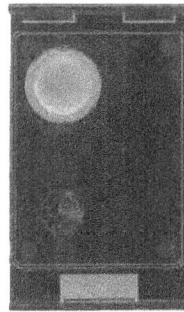

Figure 1: DT-648 Open holder with TLD card inside

(5) *Factors affecting accuracy.* The LiF TLD is not overly sensitive to environmental extremes, and does not require cold storage. However, to achieve the most accurate results, the following factors must be considered:

(a) LiF TLD cards should be kept clean. Spurious dose readings can result if the card is soiled or chemically stained. Each TLD card shall be carefully inspected upon collection, and soiled cards cleaned prior to their return for processing. Cards may be cleaned locally using a soft sponge made damp with mild detergent and water, and then rinsed with a clean, water dampened sponge. Do not use chemical solvents or cleaning fluids on LiF TLD cards. Do not mark, write, or put tape on either side of the card.

(b) Damaged cards, such as bent, broken, missing components, permanently soiled or stained, should be noted by a comment in the remarks section of the dosimetry report. The Naval Dosimetry Center can repair most types of damage and accurately evaluate the TLD provided the damage is recognized before the card is processed.

(c) Sunlight and fluorescent light can, after prolonged exposure, induce false TLD readings of up to 20 mrem (0.2 mSv). This is reported to occur if the TLD card is exposed to light for several hours while removed from the holder. Thus, bare LiF TLD cards should be stored in the dark when not in use.

(d) Static electricity or electrical discharge has been reported to have caused spurious dose readings on LiF TLD cards. This occurs only if the bare cards are subject to such treatment while removed from the holder. If it is suspected, include a comment in the remarks section of the dosimetry report.

(e) High ambient temperatures (over 115 degrees F) can cause reduced sensitivity of the LiF TLD and may result in dose evaluations being as much as 25% low. If a LiF TLD is used where the ambient temperature exceeds 115 degrees F on one or more days during the issue period, note in the remarks section of the dosimetry report "TLD# _____ exposed for _____ days to temperatures above 115 degrees F".

(f) The integrity of the card holder is critical to ensuring an accurate measurement. If a holder is damaged in a way that compromises its ability to protect the TLD card (for example, if the mylar window is torn), it can allow the TLD card inside to be damaged, exposed to light, or collect dirt. Each TLD holder shall be carefully inspected prior to issue and upon collection. A defective or damaged holder shall not be used. If a holder is discovered upon TLD collection with damage that could have affected its ability to protect the TLD card, it shall be reported in the remarks section of the NAVMED Form 6470/3, indicating which TLD card number corresponds to the damaged holder, and the nature of the damage.

(6) *Card Holder and Opener.*

(a) The card is notched in one corner, and the back of the card holder is molded so the notched card can be oriented one way only to sit flat and facilitate easy closure of the holder. With proper orientation of the card, the holder will snap shut easily. If the holder does not close easily, check for misorientation of the front and back of the holder, or for some other obstruction.

(b) To open the holder, place the opener in the slot at the top of the holder via the back, with the thumb depressor of the opener oriented toward the bottom of the holder, and press the opener to open the holder. Do not torque the opener in the slot of the card holder. See Figure 2 for proper opener orientation. Improper orientation will make opening impossible.

(7) *Wearing the DT-648.* The holder with the card enclosed should normally be worn on the front of the trunk of the body. Attachment to the front of the body can be accomplished by one of two methods (shown in Figure 3):

(a) The belt loops on the back of the card holder can be used to place it on a belt; for neutron monitoring, this is the only method authorized;

(b) An attachable strap can be used to attach it to a pocket flap or lapel. In either of the two methods, the badge holder must be positioned so the front of the holder is facing away from the body.

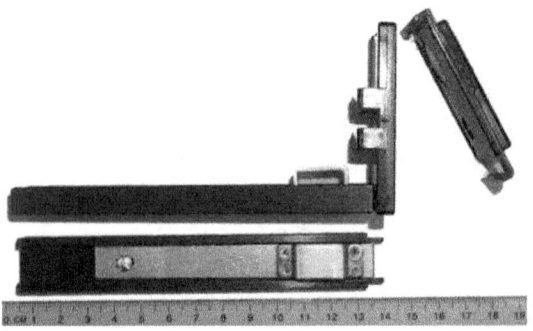

Figure 2. DT-648 Opener properly inserted into the holder for opening.

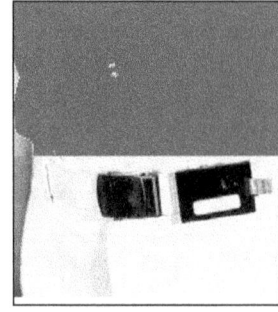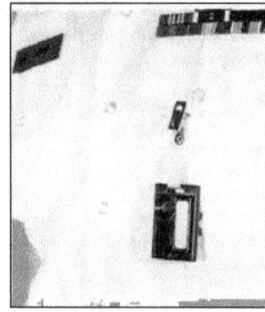

Figure 3. DT-648 DT-648 TLD shown proper usage at the waist and chest.

(8) *Issuing TLDs*

(a) In general, LiF dosimeters are issued for a period of 6 to 7 weeks (twice per quarter). The first issue period of the calendar year shall normally begin in January. The Naval Dosimetry Center will forward a new batch of TLDs every 6 weeks. These TLDs shall be issued (a new issue period begun) as soon as practicable after receipt, but in no case later than the date indicated on the shipping container. Do not mix TLD batches. All TLDs used during an issue period should be from the same batch. Inspect the TLDs upon receipt to ensure the serial numbers match those on the enclosed shipping list, and no damage has occurred in transit. Information required on the dosimetry reports shall be entered according to instructions on the reverse side of the forms or instructions in this manual, whichever is the more current. (Activities using a BUMED approved computer program shall follow the instructions provided in the program.) Special care must be taken to ensure the names of the individuals receiving the dosimeters are properly recorded, and the correct radiation type code and occupational code are assigned (see back of NAVMED Form 6470/3) to ensure proper processing and dose assignment. The issue period for the DT 648 LiF TLD shall be six to seven weeks (i.e., twice per quarter), except as provided below:

(1) For personnel assigned to fleet ballistic missile submarines, the issue period shall be for the duration of a patrol cycle. For personnel assigned to fast attack submarines, LiF TLDs may be issued on a not to exceed calendar quarterly basis.

(2) Personnel in the dosimetry program have an ongoing need for monitoring and most are issued a LiF TLD for the entire issue period, to include absences from the command during the issue period (for example, leave). For personnel issued a TLD after the start of the issue period, or who turn in a TLD before the end of the issue period (for example, due to transfer or termination), the issue and collection dates should reflect the actual period of issue. For personnel who are issued a LiF TLD for a particular job of less than 6 weeks duration or started during the regular issue period, the issue period should be for the duration of the time the TLD is actually issued to the individual for the job. For example, if the individual is issued a TLD on the 11th of the month, and

the same TLD is collected from the individual on the 23rd of the same month, the issue period is from the 11th to the 23rd of the month. A LiF TLD collected before the end of the issue period shall not be separated from the rest of the cards in issue; it should not be sent under separate cover from the batch it was shipped in; it should be kept with the rest of the batch until ready for submission to the Naval Dosimetry Center. If an individual is issued a TLD at some other time than the start of the issue period and the individual's jobs will involve exposure for the rest of the period, then the issue period shall be from the time of issue to the end of the period, including periods of leave.

(3) For personnel suspected of having exceeded an exposure limit, their LiF TLD and two control TLDs from the same batch shall be submitted for evaluation as soon as practicable. Submission of the TLDs should be coordinated with the Naval Dosimetry Center to ensure receipt and prompt processing.

(b) The issue period for posted environmental or area dosimeters, DT 648 TLDs, shall be the same as that used for personnel.

(c) The issue period will be started or stopped to allow an individual's radiation exposure record to be updated quarterly. The definition of a calendar quarter is given in Chapter 1 of this manual.

(d) If replacement dosimeters are not available at the end of the normal issue period, the issue period may be extended until new dosimeters are available. However, if an extension of the normal 6 to 7 week issue period is necessary, the Naval Dosimetry Center shall be notified by message to alert the Dosimetry Center to potential shipping and/or TLD exchange problems. A return response will not be sent unless requested. LiF TLDs shall not be kept for greater than 150 days without Naval Dosimetry Center approval.

(9) *Collecting and Submitting TLDs for Processing*

(a) At the end of the issue period, all personnel and posted/area dosimeter TLDs shall be collected, the cards removed from their holders and placed in the same numerical order as they appear on the report form, NAVMED Form 6470/3. (Activities using a BUMED approved computer program need not place the cards in any specific order if this report is submitted on magnetic media.) The cards shall be submitted to the Naval Dosimetry Center within five working days after collection unless otherwise approved by BUMED. All dosimeters from the same shipment batch shall be returned together.

(b) When removing the LiF TLD card from its holder, observe any change in orientation from the designed orientation and if the TLD card has been rotated or put in upside down, note the change in orientation in the remarks section of the NAVMED Form 6470/3. Damage to the TLD card, damage to the holder that affects its ability to protect the TLD card, or any unusual occurrence associated with the TLD card during the issue period shall be recorded in the Remarks section of the NAVMED Form

6470/3. Dirty cards shall be cleaned per paragraph 6-5(5)(a).

(c) TLD cards shall be packed in the shipping container to maintain order. Cards may be secured in the shipping container by filling voids with packing material. Do not wrap the cards or use adhesive tape or rubber bands that contact the cards.

(d) Forward an original dosimetry report, NAVMED Form 6470/3 (see Appendix A for sample) with each submission. Each shipment shall be sent via traceable means, e.g., certified mail. Each shipment of TLDs sent from the Dosimetry Center should contain a printed list of card serial numbers in that shipment; this list should be returned with the shipment when sent to the Dosimetry Center for evaluation. If an entire shipment is being returned to the Dosimetry Center unused, the shipment shall be accompanied with a memorandum indicating the TLDs were unused.

(e) If a DT-648 is used for research or other purposes so it received a dose greater than five rem, it shall be segregated from the personnel monitoring TLDs and marked for special processing. This precaution is to preclude high dosed TLDs being mistaken for personnel monitoring dosimeters. In addition, if the dosimeters have been dosed in excess of 100 rads then that should be indicated. Processing DT-648 dosimeters dosed in excess of 500 rads requires special adjustments to the processor to prevent damage and loss of glow curve information.

(10) *Control LiF TLDs.* The purpose of submitting control dosimeters with each submission group to be evaluated is to determine the amount of radiation the TLDs receive from background while they are in transit or being stored. As such, control TLDs should be stored with the unused cards in a background area, away from any existing man made radiation sources.

(a) Two control LiF TLD cards, which must be from the same batch as the issued TLDs, shall be included and designated as control cards in each submission for evaluation.

(b) Exposure from control TLDs is subtracted from the personnel/posted dosimeter exposure readings at the Naval Dosimetry Center. The value of the control listed on the exposure report form is raw exposure; the exposure listed for personnel/posted/area dosimeters is the net exposure of the card i.e., gross card readings minus the background exposure.

(11) *Storage of LiF TLDs*

(a) When issued personnel dosimeters are not being worn, they should be stored in a low background area, i.e., an area where the dosimeters are not being exposed to manmade radiation sources. Likewise, control and unissued LiF TLD cards shall be stored in an area removed from man-made radiation sources.

(b) Do not stockpile batches of TLDs. Maintaining more than one set of TLD cards is not authorized.

(12) *Dosimetry Report Forms.* The form used with the DT-648 dosimeter is the Radiation Exposure Report NAVMED Form 6470/3. The reverse side of the form has detailed instructions on how to prepare the

report for submission. After the LiF cards are evaluated, a report will be completed by the Naval Dosimetry Center and returned to the submitting activity. A copy of NAVMED Form 6470/3 is contained in Appendix A.

(13) *Changes to Program*. Changes to the local dosimetry program shall be communicated to the Naval Dosimetry Center by letter or message. Examples of the types of changes that should be communicated are:

(a) Large changes in the number of personnel monitored;

(b) Problems that affect your program;

(c) Temporary or permanent termination of the requirement for dosimetry services;

(d) Address or UIC change.

(14) *Security and Identification Stickers*. These items are for optional use determined by the customer.

(a) After the TLD card is loaded into the black holder, an optional gray sticker stating "USN Do Not Remove" may be placed in the slot at the top of the badge holder to prevent tampering. The tape cannot be removed without destroying the tape, indicative the holder may have been opened. The wearer shall be instructed not to attempt to open the holder, as the card holder may be damaged or the card misoriented.

(b) The optional identification sticker may be placed on the engraved section of the front of the black card holder. The use of different color stickers per issue period can assist in collection and distribution of the dosimeters. The identification label must never be placed directly onto the LiF card. Adhesive residue will alter the signal produced by the LiF chips when heated, producing an erroneous reading. In addition, do not write any information, i.e., the wearer's name, on the LiF card.

(c) The silver mylar window on the badge holder may become damaged or dislodged on rare occasion. If so, round silver mylar window replacements are available from the Naval Dosimetry Center upon request. The damaged window cover should be completely removed before replacing it with a new one. If the round silver mylar replacement is not available at the time of need, the gray "USN Do Not Remove" sticker can be used in the interim. Remove the damaged window and place a portion of the gray sticker on the inside of the badge holder with the adhesive facing out, covering the opening of the window. Damage to the window does not require a subsequent dose estimate to be performed.

(15) *Suspension of Dosimetry Program*. Commands may temporarily suspend personnel dosimetry during upkeep or overhaul periods as deemed operationally appropriate. If the Naval Dosimetry Center provides the dosimetry devices, indicate the projected date of program suspension to the Naval Dosimetry Center by letter. Reactivation of the personnel dosimetry program will require written communication with the Naval Dosimetry Center.

(16) *Termination of Dosimetry Programs*. To permanently terminate an existing personnel dosimetry program, submit a letter to the Naval Dosimetry Center stating the command name, UIC, and projected termination date. With the submission of the final issue of personnel dosimetry devices, include all unused/recovered TLDs, TLD holders, holder clips, and openers. Upon receipt of the final exposure information, forward a Situational Report of Occupational Exposure, NAVMED 6470/1, with remarks in block 17 indicating the program has been discontinued.

(17) *Decommissioned Vessels and Commands*. Personnel radiation exposure records including annual and situational reports, exposure investigations, worksheets, charts, calibration results and statistical summaries will be disseminated per SECNAVINST 5212.5 series.

6-6. Environmental and Area Monitoring

(1) The DT-648 can be used as a photon/beta monitor or a gamma/neutron monitor.

(a) The DT-648 card placed in its black holder can be used as a photon/beta posted dosimeter. No special mounting or phantom is required; however, the device shall be oriented so the front of the card holder faces the radiation source. The term "posted" is used with this type of monitoring.

(b) The DT-648 card placed in a polyethylene cylinder, which is essentially the same size and internal design as an AN/PDR-70, constitutes a gamma/neutron area monitor to monitor gamma and neutron radiation. This area monitor, designated as the BUMED Area Monitor (BAM) consists of the polyethylene cylinder with a drawer that holds two cards, totally encased in an aluminum box for mounting and protection. It may be used in areas where the neutron energy spectrum is not known. The BAM is the only device authorized for neutron area monitoring. The area monitor should be mounted, either by bolting or gluing, so one of the four larger surfaces faces the neutron source, and the drawer is in the horizontal plane. The drawer is manually removed when unlocked and two LiF TLD cards are inserted so the notched corners of the cards align with the positioning guide in the drawer. A special drawer is needed for use with a DT-648 area monitor. When correctly inserted, one card will have the I.D. number side down, and the other the I.D. number side up with the six digit serial number visible (see Figure 4).

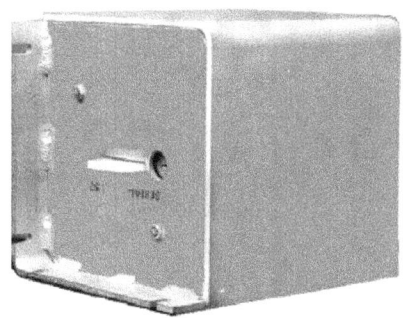

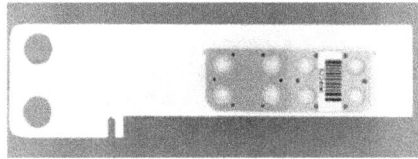

Figure 4. BUMED Area Monitor (BAM) (top) with plastic drawer showing the placement of 2 DT-648 TLD cards (bottom)

After positioning the cards, slowly slide the drawer into the phantom, close and lock. The serial numbers of the two cards must be recorded in columns 5 and 6 on the NAVMED Form 6470/3, with one serial number entered in column 5 and the other entered in column 6. Order is unimportant. The term "area monitor" is to be used only with the polyethylene cylinder. Activities required to perform neutron area monitoring may request the BAM from the Naval Dosimetry Center.

6-7. Extremity Monitoring

(1) A limited number of personnel, particularly those in nuclear medicine, radiation therapy and some industrial applications, handle large quantities of radioactive substances in the routine performance of their job. To assure appropriate radiation protection practices are followed and to evaluate exposure to extremities, the Naval Dosimetry Center provides and evaluates the EXT RAD-100 finger ring dosimeter (see Figure 5). Finger ring service may be obtained upon request to the Naval Dosimetry Center, stating the requirement, number of personnel to be monitored, location of the dosimeter on the individual, radioactive materials being handled and other pertinent information. The EXT RAD-100 is normally evaluated for exposure to photons only. Evaluation for beta exposures may be performed upon request. Instructions for handling and use of the EXT RAD-100 are provided to the customer upon approval of program implementation by the Naval Dosimetry Center.

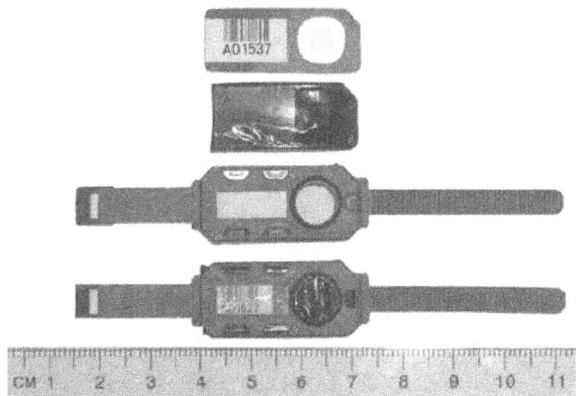

Figure 5. EXTRAD-100 Finger ring thermoluminescent dosimeters at various stages of assembly.

6-8. Accident Dosimeter

(1) The DT-518/ PD accident dosimeter (Figures 6 and 7) is a passive dosimeter which may be mounted on bulkheads or on personnel badges.

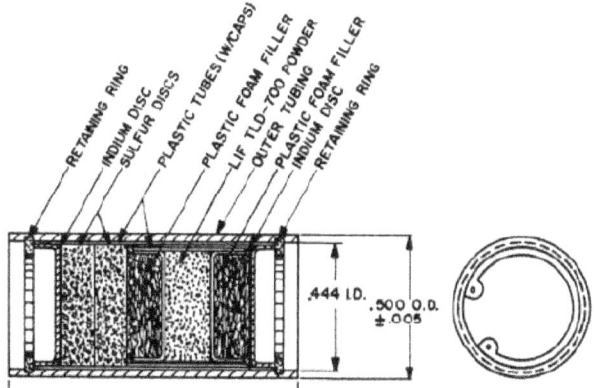

Figure 6. Illustration of the DT-518/ PD accident dosimeter with retaining rings and detector capsule.

Figure 7. Photograph of the DT-518/ PD accident dosimeter. The scale shown is in inches.

The DT-518 contains sulfur pellets, an indium foil, and thermoluminescent powder. The two sulfur pellets and indium foil are used for neutron dose determination. The thermoluminescent powder is used for gamma dose determination. The sulfur pellets and indium foil are also contained in the endcaps of the DT-526/ PD.

In the event of a high dose (accident dose) the DT-518 accident dosimeter shall be sent to the Naval Dosimetry Center for readout. The technical manual for the DT-518 accident dosimeter is NAVELEX 0967-LP-133-1010.

The DT-518 accident dosimeter measures neutron exposures from 10 to 50,000 rad and gamma ray doses from 1 to 10,000 rad.

6-9. Battlefield Dosimeters

(1) The DT-60 Navy battlefield dosimeter (Figure 8) is a passive dosimeter that uses a silver phosphate glass that darkens with exposure to high-energy gamma and thermal neutron irradiation. The dosimeter is housed in a black plastic case that is sealed with a rubber gasket.

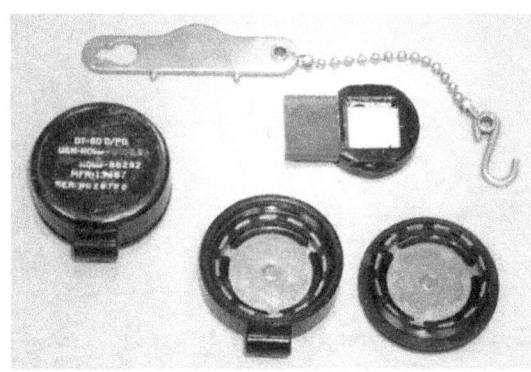

Figure 8. DT-60 battlefield dosimeter. (Top: Opener, Left: Unopened, Right: Disassembled).

The DT-60 is read in the CP-95/PD Reader. The CP-95/PD has an electronic computer indicator that runs on 110V, 60 Hz AC power. This reader is calibrated for gamma exposure. The CP-95 Reader has two scales that readout in roentgen (R) (0-200 R, 0-600 R).

(2) The DT-236 Marine Corps battlefield dosimeter (Figure 9) is designed to measure short duration, high intensity neutron and prompt gamma radiation. The dosimeter uses a wide based silicon junction diode to measure neutron radiation and a silver activated phosphate glass to measure gamma radiation. The elements are encased in a tamper resistant locket worn on the wrist.

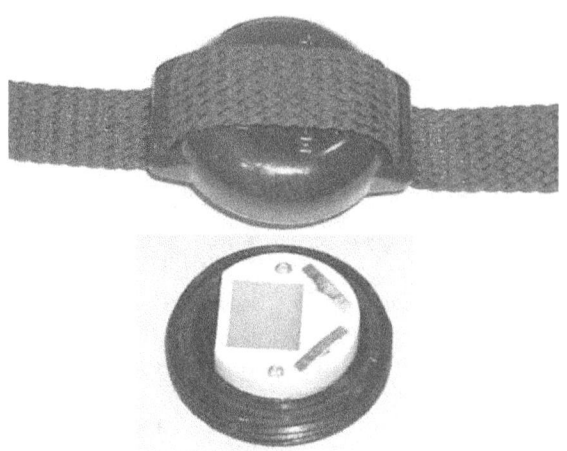

Figure 9. Marine Corps DT-236 battlefield dosimeter; (Top: On wristband, Bottom: Opened up).

The DT-236 is read with the AN/PDR-75 RADIAC set. The reader is powered by a 24 Volt DC source and uses a single digital readout to display the combined gamma and neutron dose ranging from 0 to 1000 rad. The reader takes non-destructive readings as often as desired.

The DT-236 can be used over a wide temperature range (-32° C to $+52^\circ$ C) and withstands all military environmental requirements e.g. shock, vibration, nuclear hardness and decontamination.

Chapter 7
STORAGE, HANDLING AND DISPOSAL

7-1. Introduction

(1) The storage, handling, transportation and disposal of radioactive material will be controlled so personnel will not be exposed to radiation unnecessarily and any exposures received will be maintained as low as reasonably achievable.

(2) The Director, Naval Nuclear Propulsion Program is responsible for prescribing and enforcing standards and requirements for control of radiation and radioactivity associated with the Naval Nuclear Propulsion Program (Executive Order 12344 of 1 Feb 1982). The requirements of this Chapter do not apply to the Nuclear Propulsion Program. Naval nuclear propulsion activities shall follow the requirements of the applicable NAVSEA Radiological Controls Manual.

7-2. Surveys

(1) Activities shall perform appropriate surveys to evaluate the extent of radiation levels, concentrations or quantities of radioactive material and the potential radiological hazards present to ensure compliance with the exposure limits in Chapter 4.

(2) The activity shall ensure instruments and equipment used for quantitative radiation measurements, e.g., dose rate and effluent monitoring instruments are calibrated periodically for the radiation measured.

(3) The following survey records shall be maintained indefinitely:

(a) Reports of surveys used to evaluate the release of radioactive material to the environment.

(b) Surveys indicating significant contaminating events, e.g., contamination of an area so that:

(1) If an individual had been present for 24 hours, the individual could have received an intake greater than 5 times an ALI.

(2) It caused access to the area to be restricted for greater than 24 hours, other than to allow an isotope with a half-life of less than 24 hours to decay prior to decontamination.

(c) Surveys used to determine estimates of personnel exposure.

(d) Surveys used to demonstrate compliance with the dose limits for non-radiation workers.

(e) Surveys used to demonstrate compliance with the dose limits for minors and declared pregnant women.

(f) Surveys used to demonstrate compliance with the dose limits for individual members of the general public.

(4) Other survey records shall be maintained for at least 3 years following the date of the survey.

7-3. Access Control of Areas

(1) *Unrestricted Area.* Access to an unrestricted area shall not be limited or controlled by the activity.

(2) *Radiation Area.* Access to radiation areas shall be controlled to prevent inadvertent entry by unauthorized personnel.

(3) *High Radiation Area.*

(a) Personnel will not be allowed access to high radiation areas unless appropriate dosimetric devices are worn following the criteria established in Chapter 6.

(b) One or more of the following access controls will be implemented. The controls shall be implemented in a way that does not prevent individuals from leaving a high radiation area.

(1) A control device that, upon entry into the area, causes the level of radiation to be reduced below that level at which an individual might receive a deep dose equivalent of 100 mrem (1 mSv) in 1 hour at 30 centimeters from the radiation source or from any surface from which the radiation penetrates;

(2) A control device that energizes a signal so the individual entering the high radiation area and the supervisor of the activity are made aware of the entry; or

(3) Entryways that are locked, except during periods when access to the areas is required, with positive control over each individual entry. Locked entryways must not prevent emergency exit.

(c) Control devices such as interlocks and visual or audible alarms must never be bypassed.

(d) Control of entrance or access to rooms or other areas in a hospital is not required solely because of the presence of radiation sources or patients containing radioactive material, provided there are personnel in attendance who will take the necessary precautions to prevent the exposure of individuals to radiation or radioactive material in excess of the limits established in Chapter 4 and to operate within the ALARA provisions of the Radioactive Material Permit and the activity's radiation protection program.

(4) *Very High Radiation Areas.* Adequate controls in addition to those for a high radiation area shall be implemented to ensure an individual is not able to gain unauthorized or inadvertent access to areas in which radiation levels could be encountered of 500 rads or more in 1 hour (8.33 rads per minute) at one meter from a radiation source or any surface through which the radiation penetrates.

(5) *Contaminated Areas.* Control measures such as monitoring, decontamination and isolation should be used to prevent spread of contamination to an uncontrolled area and to protect personnel in the contaminated area. If protective clothing is required, provision for donning and removing the protective clothing and masks should be available at the point of entry and egress to the contaminated areas.

(6) *Reporting Requirements for Loss of Access, Damage due to Property or Personnel Injury.* An activity shall report to the Chairman, Naval Radiation Safety Committee (OPNAV N-45) and Chief, BUMED (MED-21):

(a) Immediately by telephone or "IMMEDIATE" message but not later than 4 hours after the discovery of an event that requires immediate protective actions necessary to avoid exposures to radiation or radioactive materials that could exceed the limits in Chapter 4.

(b) Within 24 hours by telephone or "IMMEDIATE" message:

(1) Of a contaminating event that requires restricted access to the area by workers or the public for more than 24 hours by imposing additional radiological controls or by prohibiting entry into the area.

(2) Of a contaminating event that involves more than five times the ALI of the lowest inhalation class of an isotope.

(3) Of a contaminating event that has access to the area restricted for a reason other than to allow isotopes with a half-life of less than 24 hours to decay prior to decontamination.

(4) Of an event that requires unplanned medical treatment at a medical facility of an individual with spreadable radioactive contamination on the individual's clothing or body.

(5) Of a fire involving more than five times the ALI of the lowest inhalation class of an isotope.

7-4. Area Posting Requirements

(1) *Unrestricted Area.* There are no posting requirements.

(2) *Radiation Area.* Radiation areas should be posted conspicuously with signs bearing the standard radiation symbol and the words "CAUTION RADIATION AREA." Additional precautions or information such as "No Loitering," "No bunking," stay-time limits, or radiation levels may be added to the signs.

(3) *High Radiation Area.* High radiation areas shall be posted conspicuously with signs bearing the standard radiation symbol and the words "CAUTION HIGH RADIATION AREA," "NO ENTRY BY UNAUTHORIZED PERSONNEL." Additional precautions, stay-time limits, or radiation levels may be included.

(4) *Very High Radiation Area.* The entrance to a very high radiation area shall be posted with a conspicuous sign or signs bearing the standard radiation symbol and words "GRAVE DANGER, VERY HIGH RADIATION AREA."

(5) *Airborne Radioactivity Area.* Airborne radioactivity areas shall be posted conspicuously with signs bearing the standard radiation symbol and the words "CAUTION AIRBORNE RADIOACTIVITY AREA."

(6) *Exceptions to the Posting Requirements*

(a) Posting of caution signs in areas or rooms containing radioactive material is not required if the radioactive material is present for periods of less than 8 hours, and is constantly attended during these periods by an individual who takes the precautions necessary to prevent the exposure of individuals to radiation or radioactive materials in excess of the limits established in Chapter 4.

(b) Rooms or other areas in hospitals that are occupied by patients are not required to be posted with caution signs provided:

(1) The patient is being treated with sealed sources or has been treated with unsealed radioactive material in quantities less than 30 millicuries, or the measured dose rate at 1 meter from the patient is less than 5 mrem (0.05 mSv) per hour; and

(2) There are personnel in attendance who will take the necessary precautions to prevent the exposure of individuals to radiation or radioactive material in excess of the limits established in Chapter 4 and to operate within the ALARA provisions of the activity's radiation protection program.

(c) A room or area is not required to be posted with a caution sign because of the presence of a sealed source provided the radiation level at 30 centimeters from the surface of the source container or housing does not exceed 5 mrem (0.05 mSv) per hour.

7-5. Labeling of Containers

(1) Each activity shall ensure each container of licensed material bears a durable, clearly visible label bearing the radiation symbol and the words "CAUTION, RADIOACTIVE MATERIAL." The label must also provide sufficient information (such as the radionuclide(s) present, an estimate of the activity, the date on which the activity was estimated, radiation levels, and kinds of materials) to permit individuals handling or using the containers, or working in the vicinity of the containers, to take precautions to avoid or minimize exposures.

(2) Each activity shall, prior to removal or disposal of empty uncontaminated containers to unrestricted areas, remove or deface the radioactive material label or otherwise clearly indicate that the container no longer contains radioactive materials.

(3) An activity is not required to label containers:

(a) Holding radioactive material in quantities less than the quantities listed in Appendix C to Paragraphs 20.1001 through

20.2401 of Title 10, Part 20, Code of Federal Regulations; or,

(b) Holding radioactive material in concentrations less than those specified in Table 3 of Appendix B of Paragraphs 20.1001 through 20.2401 of Title 10, Part 20, Code of Federal Regulations; or,

(c) Attended by an individual who takes the precautions necessary to prevent the exposure of individuals in excess of the limits listed in Chapter 4; or,

(d) In transport and packaged and labeled per the Department of Transportation; or

(e) Used and accessible only by authorized individuals.

7-6. Storage and Control of Radioactive Materials

(1) *General.* Activities shall prevent the unauthorized removal or access to radioactive materials that are stored in controlled or unrestricted areas; and, shall control and maintain constant surveillance of radioactive material that is in a controlled or unrestricted area and that is not in storage.

(2) *Nuclear Regulatory Commission Licensed Radioactive Material.* Specific regulations covering the possession and use of Nuclear Regulatory Commission (NRC) licensed radioactive materials are contained in the Code of Federal Regulations, Title 10. The Navy has been issued a specific license of broad scope by the NRC which authorizes the Naval Radiation Safety Committee to control the possession, use, storage, and disposal of radioactive materials. The Committee will grant individual activities a Naval Radioactive Material Permit (NRMP) for the use of NRC licensed, naturally occurring, and accelerator produced material in response to an application made by OPNAVINST 6470.3. Advice and assistance is available from the appropriate technical support center as listed in OPNAVINST 6470.3.

(3) *Transfer and Accountability.* Radioactive material controlled by an NRMP may be transferred only to persons currently holding a state license or registration, NRC license or NRMP to possess the specific type and quantity of material.

7-7. Transportation, Receipt, and Reporting of Lost Radioactive Material

(1) *Transportation.* Transportation of radioactive materials should be by applicable portions of the following regulations or documents:

(a) Title 49 CFR Parts 171-179 Department of Transportation regulations for shipment by rail or highway.

(b) Title 14 CFR Part 103 Federal Aviation Agency regulations for shipment by air.

(c) Title 26 CFR Part 146-U.S. Coast Guard regulations for shipment by water.

(d) Title 39 CFR Part 15-U.S. Postal Regulation for shipment by mail.

(e) NAVSUP PUB 505 Packaging and Handling of Dangerous Materials for Transportation by Military Aircraft.

(2) *Procedures for Receiving and Opening Packages*

(a) Each activity who expects to receive a package containing quantities of radioactive material in excess of a Type A quantity, as defined in Paragraph 71.4 and Appendix A to Part 71 of Title 10 Code of Federal Regulations shall make arrangements to receive:

(1) The package when the carrier offers it for delivery; or

(2) Notification of the arrival of the package at the carrier's terminal and to take possession of the package expeditiously.

(b) Each activity shall monitor the external surfaces of a package known to contain radioactive material for radioactive contamination and radiation levels if the package:

(1) Is labeled as containing radioactive material; or

(2) Has evidence of potential contamination, such as packages that are crushed, wet, or damaged.

(c) Each activity shall perform the monitoring required by paragraph (b) of this section as soon as practicable after receipt of the package, but not later than 3 hours after the package is received at the activity's facility if it is received during the activity's normal working hours, or not later than 3 hours from the beginning of the next working day if it is received after normal working hours.

(d) The activity shall immediately notify the final delivery carrier, Chairman, Naval Radiation Safety Committee (OPNAV N45) and Chief, BUMED (MED-21) by telephone or message when:

(1) Removable radioactive surface contamination exceeds the limits of Paragraph 71.87 of Title 10, Code of Federal Regulations; or

(2) External radiation levels exceed the limits of Paragraph 71.47 of Title 10, Code of Federal Regulations.

(e) Each activity shall establish, maintain, and retain written procedures for safely opening packages in which radioactive material is received and ensure due consideration is given to special instructions for the type of package being opened.

(3) *Loss or Theft of Radioactive Material*

(a) Each activity shall report by telephone or "IMMEDIATE" message to the Chairman, Naval Radiation Safety Committee (OPNAV N-45) and Chief, BUMED (MED-21), immediately after its occurrence becomes known, any lost, stolen, or missing radioactive material in an aggregate quantity equal to or greater than 1,000 times the quantity specified in Appendix C to Paragraphs 20.1001 through 20.2401 of Title 10 Part 20 of the Code of Federal Regulations under such circumstances it appears to the activity an exposure could result to persons in unrestricted areas. A written report shall follow within 30 days.

(b) Each activity shall report within 30 days after the occurrence of any lost, stolen, or missing radioactive material becomes known to the activity in a quantity equal to or greater than 10 times the quantity specified in Appendix C to

Paragraphs 20.1001 to 20.2401 of Title 10 Part 20 of the Code of Federal Regulations.

(c) The written report shall contain the following information:

(1) A description of the licensed material involved, including kind, quantity, and chemical and physical form; and,

(2) A description of the circumstances under which the loss or theft occurred; and,

(3) A statement of disposition, or probable disposition, of the radioactive material involved; and,

(4) Exposures of individuals to radiation, circumstances under which the exposures occurred, and the possible total effective dose equivalent to persons in unrestricted areas; and,

(5) Actions that have been taken to recover the material; and,

(6) Procedures or measures that have been, or will be, adopted to ensure against a recurrence of the loss or theft of radioactive material.

(4) *Management of Irradiated or Contaminated Personnel* Information concerning management of irradiated or contaminated personnel including personnel decontamination procedures may be obtained from BUMEDINST 6470.10 series or the appropriate NAVSEA Manual or from the Technical Support Centers listed in OPNAVINST 6470.3.

7-8. Waste Disposal

(1) Improper disposal of radioactive waste presents potential hazards to the public. Regulations issued by the Nuclear Regulatory Commission contain certain requirements which must be met by persons disposing of radioactive material which has reached the end of its useful life. The Naval Radiation Safety Committee has established a centrally managed low level radioactive waste (LLRW) disposal program that uses an interservice support agreement with the Department of the Army for consolidation, compaction and burial of LLRW. Navy and Marine Corps activities shall use this program for radioactive waste disposal unless an alternate method is authorized by their Naval Radioactive Materials Permit (NRMP) or by the Chairman, Naval Radiation Safety Committee (OPNAV N-45).

(a) *Procedures.* Commands shall dispose of radioactive material per Title 10 Code of Federal Regulations and their NRMP.

(1) Activities shall dispose of radioactive material by:

(a) Transfer to a Nuclear Regulatory Commission authorized recipient;

(b) Decay in storage; or

(c) Release in effluents within the limits of Paragraph 20.1301 of Title 10 Part 20, Code of Federal Regulations.

(2) Materials which cannot be disposed of by the above methods shall be disposed of by using the LLRW disposal program. The technical support center conducting this program is NAVSEA Detachment, Radiological Affairs Support Office (NAVSEADET RASO), Yorktown, VA. Radiation safety officers shall contact RASO directly for procedures and instructions. Do not ship radioactive materials for disposal without RASO authorization.

(3) Navy and Marine Corps personnel are prohibited from accepting radioactive material from civilians, civilian institutions or other Government agencies for the purpose of waste disposal.

(b) *Records.* Commands shall maintain records of disposal of radioactive material per Title 10 Code of Federal Regulations, the command's NRMP or NAVSEA Instructions as appropriate.

APPENDIX A

SAMPLE FORMS

RECORD OF OCCUPATIONAL EXPOSURE TO IONIZING RADIATION

1. NAME (Last, First, Middle Initial)	2. SOC. SEC. NUMBER	3. RANK/RATE/GRADE	4. DATE OF BIRTH

INDIVIDUAL'S		PERIOD OF EXPOSURE		DOSE EQUIVALENT THIS PERIOD (rem)					ACCUMULATED DOSE (rem)	INITIALS
Activity 5	Occ Code 6	From (YYYYMMDD) 7	To (YYYYMMDD) 8	Shallow Dose Equiv. 9	Deep Dose Equiv. Photon 10	Deep Dose Equiv. Neutron 11	Committed Effective Dose Equiv. 12	Total Effective Dose Equiv. 13	Lifetime Total Effective Dose Equiv. 14	Person Making Entry 15

16. REMARKS (Continue on additional sheet(s) if necessary)

TO BE RETAINED PERMANENTLY IN INDIVIDUAL'S HEALTH RECORD

NAVMED FORM 6470/10 (4/1999)

INSTRUCTIONS FOR PREPARATION OF NAVMED FORM 6470/10

ITEM

1. Enter the last name, first name and middle initial. Separate each component of the name with a space. If the full name exceeds 40 spaces, truncate after the 40th space.

2. Enter Social Security Number, e.g., 000-00-0000. If the individual does not have a social security number, i.e., a foreign national, enter a pseudo SSN as: 800 for the first 3 digits, the year, month, and day of birth. (i.e., 800-YY-MMDD)

3. Enter, in not more than 10 spaces, the rank/rate/grade the individual possesses when initiating this form. This item need not be updated until a new NAVMED FORM 6470/10 is initiated. Use standard military/civil service abbreviations, e.g., CAPT, COL, MAJ, HMCS, MM2, SSGT, LCPL, GS9, WG5, etc. Abbreviate civilian titles as necessary, e.g., Radiological Physicist to Rad Phys; Electrical Welder to Elec Wldr, etc.

4. Enter date of birth by 4 digit year, month, and day using no spaces and all capitals, e.g., 1975APR13.

5. Enter the name of the activity or unit. The activity's / unit's abbreviated name or ship hull number(s) may be used. The activity should represent either the activity or unit where the individual is permanently assigned or, if TAD, where the exposure occurred.

6. Occupation Codes:

10 Nuc. Propl. (Rad. Worker)	20 Weapons (Rad. Worker)	30 Medical (Diagnostics)	40 Gamma Radiographer
11 Nuc. Propl. (Non-Rad.)	21 Weapons (Non-Rad.)	31 Dental	41 X-ray Radiography and
12 Nuc. Propl. (Visitor)	22 Weapons (Visitor)	32 Medical (Nuc. Med.)	Accel. Radiography <10 MeV
		33 Medical (Therapy)	42 Accel. Radiography => 10 MeV
50 Research			43 RADIAC Calibration
51 Research (Isotopes)	90 Other		44 General Industrial

7. Enter the 4 digit year, month, and day the exposure period began using no spaces and all capitals, e.g., 1999JAN04.

8. Enter the 4 digit year, month, and day the exposure period ended, e.g., 1999FEB15.

Note: For items 9 – 14, enter radiation doses received in rem to three decimal places, i.e., 03.450. Enter doses evaluated as zero as 00.000. Do not use 'X's'or the term minimal. If not monitored, leave blank. Do not enter 00.000 for radiation types not specifically monitored.

9. Enter *shallow dose equivalent*, which is the external exposure to the skin at a tissue depth of 0.007 centimeters or 7 milligrams per centimeters squared. If shallow dose equivalent was not monitored, leave blank.

10. Enter *deep dose equivalent* photon, which is external exposure from photon radiations (x and gamma rays) to the whole body at a tissue depth of 1 centimeter or 1000 milligrams per centimeter squared.

11. Enter *deep dose equivalent* neutron, which is external exposure from neutron radiation to the whole body at a tissue depth of 1 centimeter or 1000 milligrams per centimeter squared.

12. Enter the *committed effective dose equivalent*, which is exposure from internally deposited radionuclide(s).

13. Enter the *total effective dose equivalent*, which is the sum of the deep dose equivalents for external exposure (items 10 & 11) and the committed effective dose equivalent for internal exposure (item 12). The total effective dose equivalent does not include the shallow dose equivalent for external exposure (item 9).

14. Enter the *lifetime total effective dose equivalent*, which is the summation of the individual's total effective dose equivalents. That is, add item 13 to the previous item 14. If item 14 is being updated from a DD 1141, then item 13 is added to the previous item 14 (Total Lifetime Exposure).

15. Initials of person making line entry. The associated name and title of each individual initialing item 15 will be recorded in the remarks section (item 16), e.g., JD - John Daniels, HMC, USN, RB - Robert Bums, 1LT, USA.

16. Enter other pertinent information, e.g., estimated exposure, skin contamination, the name and title of individual(s) initialing item 15, annotation(s) to correct administrative errors on the NAVMED FORM 6470/10, etc.

Note: This record is required for all individuals who have been or are being monitored for exposure to ionizing radiation. It shall be filed in the individual's health record, where it shall be retained permanently.

RECORD OF OCCUPATIONAL EXPOSURE TO IONIZING RADIATION FROM INTERNALLY DEPOSITED RADIONUCLIDES

1. NAME (Last, First, Middle Initial)				2. SOC. SEC. NUMBER	3. RANK/RATE/GRADE		4. DATE OF BIRTH	

Individual's Activity 5	Date (YYYYMMMDD) 6	Time 7	Anatomical Location or Sample Monitored 8	Detector's MDA (nCi) 9	Radio-Nuclide 10	Amount Detected (nCi) 11	Committed Effective Dose Equivalent (rem) 12	Initials Of Person Making Entry 13

16. REMARKS (Continue on additional sheet(s) if necessary)

TO BE RETAINED PERMANENTLY IN INDIVIDUAL'S HEALTH RECORD

NAVMED FORM 6470/11 (4/1999)

INSTRUCTIONS FOR PREPARATION OF NAVMED FORM 6470/11

<u>ITEM</u>

1. Enter the last name, first name and middle initial. If the full name exceeds 40 spaces, truncate after the 40th space.

2. Enter Social Security Number, e.g., 000-00-0000. If the individual does not have a social security number, i.e., a foreign national, enter a pseudo SSN as: 800 for the first 3 digits, the year, month, and day of birth. (i.e., 800-YY-MMDD)

3. Enter, in not more than 10 spaces, the rank/rate/grade the individual possesses when initiating this form. This item need not be updated until a new NAVMED FORM 6470/11 is initiated. Use standard military / civil service abbreviations, e.g., CAPT, HMCS, MM2, SSGT, LCPL, GS9, WG5, etc. Abbreviate civilian titles as necessary, e.g., Radiological Physicist to Rad Phys; Electrical Welder to Elec Wldr, etc.

4. Enter date of birth by 4 digit year, month, and day using no spaces and all capitals, e.g., 1975APR13.

5. Enter the name of the activity or unit. The activity's / unit's abbreviated name or ship hull number(s) may be used. The activity should represent either the activity or unit where the individual is permanently assigned or, if TAD, where the exposure occurred.

6. Enter the 4 digit year, month, and day of monitoring using no spaces and all capitals, e.g., 1999JAN04.

7. When required, enter the military time of day when monitoring was performed, e.g., 1410.

8. Enter the anatomical location or type of sample monitored, e.g., chest, thyroid, abdomen, feces, urine.

9. Enter the minimum detectable activity (MDA) of the counting system at the 95% or higher confidence level in nanocuries (nCi).

10. Enter the radionuclide monitored for or detected, e.g., Co-60, I-131. If more than one radionuclide is monitored for or detected, list the radionuclides on successive lines. Items 5-9 do not need to be repeated when reporting multiple radionuclides.

11. Enter the amount of activity detected in nanocuries (nCi). If the resultant activity is less than MDA, enter < MDA.

12. Enter the *committed effective dose equivalent* in rem, which is occupational exposure from internally deposited radionuclide(s). The committed effective dose equivalent will be calculated by a BUMED approved facility (see NAVMED P-5055).

13. Initials of person making line entry. The associated name and title of each individual initialing item 13 will be recorded in the remarks section (item 14), e.g., JD - John Daniels, HMC, USN.

14. Enter any remarks or explanatory comments, e.g., abnormal radionuclides detected, method of calculation, etc.

EXPOSURE TO IONIZING RADIATION

REPORT OF PERSONNEL EXPOSURE TO IONINZING RADIATION — ANNUAL __ SITUATIONAL __

REPORT OF PERSONNEL EXCEEDING RADIATION EXPOSURE LIMITS

(REPORT SYMBOL MED 6470-1)
(REPORT SYMBOL MED 6470-2)

1. ACTIVITY SUBMITTING REPORT (Name and Address)

2. UIC

3. CALENDAR YEAR REPORTED

4. DATE PREPARED

MEMBER'S INFORMATION

| Name (Last, First, Middle Initial) 5 | Social Security Number 6 | Date Of Birth YYYYMMDD 7 | Occ Code 8 | PERIOD OF EXPOSURE | | DOSE EQUIVALENT THIS PERIOD (rem) | | | | | ACCUMULATED (rem) |
				From YYYYMMDD 9	To YYYYMMDD 10	Shallow Dose Equiv. 11	Deep Dose Equiv. Photon 12	Deep Dose Equiv. Neutron 13	Committed Effective Dose Equiv. 14	Total Effective Dose Equiv. 15	Lifetime Total Effective Dose Equiv. 16

17. REMARKS (Continue on additional sheet(s) if necessary)

18. Signature (Individual Preparing Report)

19. APPROVED (Radiation Health Officer, Medical Officer, or Approving Authority)

TITLE:

NAVMED FORM 6470/1 (4/1999)

Page ____ of ____

INSTRUCTIONS FOR PREPARATION OF NAVMED 6470/1
Personnel Exposure to Ionizing Radiation (Report symbol MED) 6470- 1)
Personnel Exceeding Radiation Exposure Limits (Report Symbol MED 6470-2)

1. General

a.   This dual purpose form may be used for either report but the reports must not be combined on the same form.

b.   These reports are required on all personnel in the Naval Establishment who have been or are being monitored for exposure to Ionizing Radiation. It shall be the responsibility of each activity of the Naval Establishment having personnel monitored to submit these reports (both paper copy and diskette) to the Naval Dosimetry Center per the following time periods. Retain a copy for your records.

   1.   NAVMED 6470/1 - Report of Personnel Exposure to Ionizing Radiation shall be submitted annually to the Naval Dosimetry Center, prior to 1 April or within 30 days of receipt of final annual exposure information (whichever is later) and shall include all personnel on board 31 December who were monitored for such exposure at any time during the calendar year at the reporting activity.

   2. NAVMED 6470/1 - Report of Personnel Exposure to Ionizing Radiation must also be prepared and submitted as a situational report if an individual so monitored was transferred, or terminated employment during the calendar year. This report shall be submitted to the Naval Dosimetry Center within 30 days of receipt of final exposure information for such transfer or termination. Data shall be obtained from the individual's Record of Occupational Exposure to Ionizing Radiation.

   3. NAVMED 6470/2 - Report of Personnel Exceeding Radiation Exposure Limits is required on all personnel in the Naval Establishment who have exceeded radiation exposure limits. It shall be the responsibility of the activity at which the limits were exceeded to submit this report to BUMED, Undersea Medicine and Radiation Health Division. A copy of the report shall be attached to each individual's NAVMED FORM 6470/10 for permanent retention. If personnel have received a dose of more then 3 rem in any one calendar quarter, the report shall be forwarded within 30 days from the determination of such exposure. If personnel have received a dose of more than 5 rem in a single incident, a report shall be forwarded within 24 hours from the determination of such exposure. If any individual has received a dose of more than 25 rem in a single incident, Chief, Bureau of Medicine and Surgery, shall be notified immediately by immediate message or telephone.

2. Specific Coding Instructions (see NAVMED P-5055, Chapter 5, for additional information)

a. Check the appropriate boxes to indicate which report is being submitted and if the report being submitted is an annual or situational report.

b. Item.
   1.   Enter name and address of reporting activity.
   2.   Enter UIC.
   3.   Enter calendar year reported.
   4.   Enter date reported.
   5.   Enter name as currently carried on rolls - last name, first name, and middle initial as appropriate. If this combination exceeds 40 spaces, truncate name at 40 characters.
   6.   Enter individual's social security account number. Enter social security number, e.g., 000-00-0000. If the individual does not have a social security number, i.e., a foreign national, enter a pseudo SSN as: 800 for the first 3 digits, the year, month, and day of birth. (i.e., 800-YY-MMDD)
   7.   Enter individual's year and month of birth.
   8.   Enter occupation code in which the majority of exposure occurred (see NAVMED P-5055, chapter 5, for occupation codes)
   9.   Enter 4 digit year, month and day monitoring period was considered to have started using no spaces, i.e., 19991027.
   10. Enter 4 digit year, month and day monitoring period was considered to have ended using no spaces, i.e., 19991226.

Note: For items 11 – 16, enter radiation doses received in rem to three decimal places, i.e., 03.450. Enter doses evaluated as zero as 00.000. Do not use 'X's'or the term minimal. If not monitored, leave blank. Do not enter 00.000 for radiation types not specifically monitored.

   11. Enter shallow dose equivalent.
   12. Enter deep dose equivalent photon.
   13. Enter deep dose equivalent neutron dose.
   14. Enter the committed effective dose equivalent.
   15. Enter total effective dose equivalent accumulated for this period; sum of items 12, 13, and 14.
   16. Enter the accumulated total lifetime dose equivalent.
   17, 18, 19 are self-explanatory.

Reporting Procedures are explained in detail in Chapter 5 of NAVMED P-5055, Radiation Health Protection Manual.

REPORT OF MEDICAL EXAMINATION

1. LAST NAME - FIRST NAME - MIDDLE NAME	2. GRADE AND COMPONENT OR POSITION	3. IDENTIFICATION NO.

4. HOME ADDRESS (Number, street or RFD, city or town, State and ZIP Code)	5. PURPOSE OF EXAMINATION Ionizing Radiation Work ( )	6. DATE OF EXAMINATION

7. SEX	8. RACE	9. TOTAL YEARS GOVERNMENT SERVICE		10. AGENCY	11. ORGANIZATION UNIT
		MILITARY	CIVILIAN		

12. DATE OF BIRTH	13. PLACE OF BIRTH	14. NAME, RELATIONSHIP, AND ADDRESS OF NEXT OF KIN

15. EXAMINING FACILITY OR EXAMINER, AND ADDRESS	16. OTHER INFORMATION

17. RATING OR SPECIALTY	TIME IN THIS CAPACITY (Total)	LAST SIX MONTHS

CLINICAL EVALUATION

NOTES: (Describe every abnormality in detail. Enter pertinent item number before each comment. Continue in item 73 and use additional sheets if necessary)

NOR-MAL	(Check each item in appropriate column, enter "NE" if not evaluated.)	ABNOR-MAL
	18. HEAD, FACE, NECK AND SCALP	
	19. NOSE	
	20. SINUSES	
	21. MOUTH AND THROAT	
	22. EARS-GENERAL (INTERNAL CANALS) (Auditory) acuity under items 70 and 71)	
	23. DRUMS (Perforation)	
	24. EYES-GENERAL (Visual acuity and refraction under items 59, 60 and 67)	
	25. OPHTHALMOSCOPIC-	
	26. PUPILS (Equality and reaction)	
	27. OCULAR MOTILITY (Associated parallel movements nystagmus)	
	28. LUNGS AND CHEST (Include breasts)	
	29. HEART (Thrust, size, rhythm, sounds)	
	30. VASCULAR SYSTEM (Varicosities, etc.)	
	31. ABDOMEN AND VISCERA (Include hernia)	
	32. ANUS AND RECTUM (Hemorrhoids, Fistulas) (Prostate, if indicated)	
	33. ENDOCRINE SYSTEM	
	34. G-U SYSTEM	
	35. UPPER EXTREMITIES (Strength, range of motion)	
	36. FEET	
	37. LOWER EXTREMITIES (Except feet) (Strength, range of motion)	
	38. SPINE, OTHER MUSCULOSKELETAL	
	39. IDENTIFYING BODY MARKS, SCARS, TATTOOS	
	40. SKIN, LYMPHATICS	
	41. NEUROLOGIC (Equilibrium tests under item 72)	
	42. PSYCHIATRIC (Specify any personality deviation)	
	43. PELVIC (Females only) (Check how done) ☐ VAGINAL ☐ RECTAL	

(Continue in Item 73)

44. DENTAL (Place appropriate symbols, shown in examples, above or below number of upper and lower teeth.)

	0				/				x				x x x				(x)			
	1 2 3	Restorable	1 2 3	Non-	1 2 3	Missing	x x x	Replaced	1 2 3	Fixed	
	32 31 30	Teeth	32 31 30	Restorable	32 31 30	Teeth	1 2 3	by	1 2 3	Partial	
	0			Teeth			32 31 30	Dentures	32 31 30	dentures	
			/		x		x x x		(x)	

RIGHT | 1 | 2 | 3 | 4 | 5 | 6 | 7 | 8 | 9 | 10 | 11 | 12 | 13 | 14 | 15 | 16 | LEFT
| 32 | 31 | 30 | 29 | 28 | 27 | 26 | 25 | 24 | 23 | 22 | 21 | 20 | 19 | 18 | 17 |

REMARKS AND ADDITIONAL DENTAL DEFECTS AND DISEASES

LABORATORY FINDINGS

45. URINALYSIS: A. SPECIFIC GRAVITY	46. CHEST X-RAY (Place, date, film number and result)
B. ALBUMIN	D. MICROSCOPIC	
C. SUGAR	

47. SEROLOGY (Specify test used and result)	48. EKG	49. BLOOD TYPE AND RH FACTOR	50. OTHER TESTS

NSN 7540-00-634-4038
88-122

Standard Form 88 (Rev. 3-89) EF
General Services Administration
Interagency Comm. on Medical Records
FIRMR (41 CFR) 201-45.505
NAVMED Overprint 6470/12 (7-01)

MEASUREMENTS AND OTHER FINDINGS

51. HEIGHT	52. WEIGHT	53. COLOR HAIR	54. COLOR EYES	55. BUILD:				56. TEMPERATURE
				☐ SLENDER	☐ MEDIUM	☐ HEAVY	☐ OBESE	

57.	BLOOD PRESSURE (Arm at heart level)					58.	PULSE (Arm at heart level)			
A. SITTING	SYS.	B. RECUMBENT	SYS.	C. STANDING (5 min.)	SYS.	A. SITTING	B. AFTER EXERCISE	C. 2 MIN. AFTER	D. RECUMBENT	E. AFTER STANDING 3 MIN.
	DIAS.		DIAS.		DIAS.					

59.	DISTANT VISION	60.		REFRACTION			61.		NEAR VISION	
RIGHT 20/	CORR. TO 20/	BY		S.		CX			CORR. TO	BY
LEFT 20/	CORR. TO 20/	BY		S.		CX			CORR. TO	BY

62. HETEROPHORIA (Specify distance)

ES°	EX°	R.H.	L.H.	PRISM DIV.	PRISM CONV. CT	PC	PD

63.	ACCOMMODATION	64. COLOR VISION (Test used and result)	65. DEPTH PERCEPTION (Test used and score)	UNCORRECTED
RIGHT	LEFT			CORRECTED

66. FIELD OF VISION	65. NIGHT VISION (Test used and score)	66. RED LENS TEST	69. INTRAOCULAR TENSION

70.	HEARING		71.						AUDIOMETER				72. PSYCHOLOGICAL AND PSYCHOMOTOR (Test used and score)
RIGHT WV	/15 SV	/15		250 256	500 512	1000 1024	2000 2048	3000 2896	4000 4096	6000 6144	8000 8192	
LEFT WV	/15 SV	/15	RIGHT									
			LEFT									

73. NOTES (Continued) AND SIGNIFICANT OR INTERVAL HISTORY

(Use additional sheets if necessary)

74. SUMMARY OF DEFECTS AND DIAGNOSES (List diagnosis with item numbers)

75. RECOMMENDATIONS-FURTHER SPECIALIST EXAMINATIONS INDICATED (Specify)	76.	A. PHYSICAL PROFILE					
		P	U	L	H	E	S

77. EXAMINEE (Check)   PQ/NPQ for Ionizing Radiation Work (   )

A. ☐ IS QUALIFIED FOR

B. ☐ IS NOT QUALIFIED FOR

B. PHYSICAL CATEGORY

78. IF NOT QUALIFIED, LIST DISQUALIFYING DEFECTS BY ITEM NUMBER	A	B	C	E

79. TYPED OR PRINTED NAME OF PHYSICIAN	SIGNATURE

80. TYPED OR PRINTED NAME OF PHYSICIAN	SIGNATURE

81. TYPED OR PRINTED NAME OF DENTIST OR PHYSICIAN (Indicate which)	SIGNATURE

82. TYPED OR PRINTED NAME OR REVIEWING OFFICER OR APPROVING AUTHORITY	SIGNATURE	NUMBER OF ATTACHED SHEETS

APPROVED
OFFICE OF MANAGEMENT AND BUDGET No. 29-R0191

REPORT OF MEDICAL HISTORY
(THIS INFORMATION IS FOR OFFICIAL AND MEDICALLY - CONFIDENTIAL USE ONLY AND WILL NOT BE RELEASED TO UNAUTHORIZED PERSONS)

1. LAST NAME-FIRST NAME-MIDDLE NAME	2. SOCIAL SECURITY OR IDENTIFICATION NO.

3. HOME ADDRESS *(Number, street or RFD, city or town, State and Zip Code)*	4. POSITION *(title, grade, component)*

5. PURPOSE OF EXAMINATION Ionizing Radiation Work ( )	6. DATE OF EXAMINATION	7. EXAMINING FACILITY OR EXAMINER, AND ADDRESS

8. STATEMENT OF EXAMINEE'S PRESENT HEALTH AND MEDICATIONS CURRENTLY USED *(Follow by description of past history, if complaint exists)*

9. HAVE YOU EVER *(Please check each item)*

YES	NO	*(Check each item)*
		Lived with anyone who had tuberculosis
		Coughed up blood
		Bled excessively after injury or tooth extraction
		Attempted suicide
		Been a sleepwalker

10. DO YOU *(Please check each item)*

YES	NO	*(Check each item)*
		Wear glasses or contact lenses
		Have vision in both eyes
		Wear a hearing aid
		Stutter or stammer habitually
		Wear a brace or back support

11. HAVE YOU EVER HAD OR HAVE YOU NOW *(Please check at left of each)*

YES	NO	DON'T KNOW	*(Check each item)*	YES	NO	DON'T KNOW	*(Check each item)*	YES	NO	DON'T KNOW	*(Check each item)*
			Scarlet fever, erysipelas				Cramps in your legs				"Trick" or locked knee
			Rheumatic fever				Frequent indigestion				Foot trouble
			Swollen or painful joints				Stomach, liver or intestinal trouble				Neuritis
			Frequent or severe headache				Gall bladder trouble or gallstones				Paralysis (including infantile)
			Dizziness or fainting spells				Jaundice or hepatitis				Epilepsy or fits
			Eye trouble				Adverse reaction to serum, drug, or medicine				Car, train, sea or air sickness
			Ear, nose or throat trouble				Broken bones				Frequent trouble sleeping
			Hearing loss				Tumor, growth, cyst, cancer				Depression or excessive worry
			Chronic or frequent colds				Rupture/hernia				Loss of memory or amnesia
			Severe tooth or gum trouble				Piles or rectal disease				Nervous trouble of any sort
			Sinusitis				Frequent or painful urination				Periods of unconsciousness
			Hay Fever				Bed wetting since age 12				Occupational or accidental exposure to ionizing radiation above Table III limits
			Head Injury				Kidney Stone or blood in urine				
			Skin diseases				Sugar or albumin in urine				Cancer or precancerous lesions
			Thyroid trouble				VD--Syphilis, gonorrhea, etc.				Anemia
			Tuberculosis				Recent gain or loss of weight				Work involving the handling of unsealed radium sources or other unsealed sources
			Asthma				Arthritis, Rheumatism, or Bursitis				
			Shortness of breath				Bone, joint or other deformity				
			Pain of pressure in chest				Lameness				
			Chronic cough				Loss of finger or toes				
			Palpitation or pounding heart				Painful or "trick" shoulder or elbow	**12. FEMALES ONLY: HAVE YOU EVER**			
			Heart trouble				Recurrent back pain				Been treated for a female disorder
			High or low blood pressure				Radiation therapy				Had a change in menstrual pattern
			Radiopharmaceuticals received for therapeutic or experimental purposes								

13. WHAT IS YOUR USUAL OCCUPATION?	14. ARE YOU *(Check one)* ☐ Right handed ☐ Left handed

YES	NO	CHECK EACH ITEM YES OR NO. EVERY ITEM CHECKED YES MUST BE FULLY EXPLAINED IN BLANK SPACE ON RIGHT
		15. Have you been refused employment or been unable to hold a job or stay in school because of:
		A: Sensitivity to chemicals, dust, sunlight, etc.
		B. Inability to perform certain motions.
		C. Inability to assume certain positions.
		D. Other medical reasons *(If yes, give reasons.)*
		16. Have you ever been treated for a mental condition? *(If yes, specify when, where, and give details.)*
		17. Have you ever been denied life insurance? *(If yes, state reason and give details.)*
		18. Have you had, or have you been advised to have, any operations? *(if yes, describe and give age at which occurred.)*
		19. Have you ever been a patient in any type of hospital? *(If yes, specify when, where why, and name of doctor and complete address of the hospital.)*
		20. Have you ever had any illness or injury other than those already noted? *(if yes, specify when, where, and give details.)*
		21. Have you consulted or been treated by clinics, physicians, healers, or other practitioners within the past 5 years for other than minor illnesses? *(if yes, give complete address of doctor, hospital, clinic, and details.)*
		22. Have you ever been rejected for military service because of physical, mental, or other reasons? *(If yes, give date and reason for rejection.)*
		23. Have you ever been discharged from military service because of physical, mental, or other reasons? *(if yes, give date, reason, and type of discharge: whether honorable, other than honorable, for unfitness or unsuitability.)*
		24. Have you ever received, is there pending, or have you applied for pension or compensation for existing disability? *(If yes specify what kind, granted by whom, and what amount, when, why.)*

I certify that I have reviewed the foregoing information supplied by me and that it is true and complete to the best of my knowledge. I authorize any of the doctors, hospitals, or clinics mentioned above to furnish the Government a complete transcript of my medical record for purposes of processing my application for this employment

TYPED OR PRINTED NAME OR EXAMINEE	SIGNATURE

NOTE: HAND TO THE DOCTOR OR NURSE, OR IF MAILED MARK ENVELOPE "TO BE OPENED BY MEDICAL OFFICER ONLY."
25. Physician's summary and elaboration of all pertinent data *(Physician's shall comment on all positive answers in items 9 through 24. Physician may develop by interview any additional medical history he deems important, and record any significant findings here.)*

TYPED OR PRINTED NAME OF PHYSICIAN OR EXAMINER	DATE	SIGNATURE	NUMBER OF ATTACHED SHEETS

*U.S. Government Printing Office: 1989- 241- 175/80263

Instructions
1. See reverse side before completing this form
2. Submit Original of this form with each submission of TLD to Naval Dosimetry Center,
   NEHC Detachment, Bethesda, MD 20889-5614.

RADIATION EXPOSURE REPORT

1. ACTIVITY SUBMITTING REPORT (Name, Address, and Telephone Number)	2. UIC	3. DATE SUBMITTED

MEMBER'S INFORMATION			EXPOSURE PERIOD INFORMATION					DOSE EVALUATION				
4. Name (Last, First, Middle Initial)	5. Soc. Sec. Number	6. TLD Number	7. Issued YYYY MMM DD	Collected YYYY MMM DD	8. Rad Type	9. Occ Code	10. Shallow Dose Equiv.	11. Deep Dose Equiv. Photon	12. Deep Dose Equiv. Neutron	13. Total Effective Dose Equiv.	14. Extremity

15. REMARKS

16. SUBMITTED BY	17. DATE RECEIVED	18. DATE RELEASED	19. APPROVED BY	PAGE ___ OF ___

NAVMED FORM 6470/3 (4/1999)

INSTRUCTIONS FOR PREPARATION OF NAVMED 6470/3

The following instructions are applicable to the numbered items on the other side of this form. TLD cards submitted for evaluation shall be listed in the following order: CONTROL TLD Cards first, followed by all TLD Cards issued to personnel, then by POSTED TLD Cards, then by BUMED AREA MONITOR (BAM) TLD Cards, and finally all UNUSED TLD Cards.

The TLD cards do not have to be submitted to the NAVDOSCEN in the same order as they are listed on the NAVMED 6470/3 if this report is submitted on magnetic media (e.g., generated by SAMS, ARCMIS, and RER computer programs.).

ITEM

1. List complete name, mailing address, and telephone number of submitting activity.
2. List five digit Unit Identification Code (UIC).
3. Record date on which the report is submitted.
4. The following entries are required in block (4): "CONTROL" for control TLD cards; last name, first name and middle initial for TLD cards issued to personnel; "POSTED" for posted TLD cards; "BAM-followed by serial number of BUMED area monitor, e.g. BAM-500," for BUMED area monitor TLD cards (Do not list the physical location of the area monitors.); and 'UNUSED' for any TLD cards not used.
5. List social security number (SSN) for all personnel to whom TLD cards were issued. If the individual does not have a social security number, i.e., a foreign national, enter a pseudo SSN as: 800 for the first 3 digits, the year, month, and day of birth. (i.e., 800-YY-MMDD) Leave blank for CONTROL, POSTED, and UNUSED TLD cards. List the serial number of the first TLD card placed in the BUMED area monitor.
6. List the serial number of the TLD card issued. List the serial number of the second TLD card placed in the BUMED area monitor.
7. List dates of issue and collection for each dosimeter in the following format YYYYMMDD.
8. Use one of the following numeric codes to indicate the type of radiation exposure to be evaluated for each dosimeter:
   1. Deep Photon
   2. Deep Neutron
   3. Deep Photon. Deep Neutron
   4. Shallow Photon and/or Beta
   5. Shallow Photon and/or Beta; Deep Photon
   6. Shallow Photon and/or Beta; Deep Photon; and Deep Neutron
   7. Extremity High Energy Photon (>70 keV)
   8. Extremity Low Energy Photon (<= 70 keV)
   9. Extremity Beta
9. Use one of the following numerical codes to indicate the occupation (occ) code of the person issued the TLD card or for TLD cards not issued to personnel:

00 Control	31 Dental
01 Posted	32 Medical (Nuclear Medicine.)
02 Area Monitor	33 Medical (Therapy)
03 Unused	40 Gamma Radiographer
10 Nuclear Propulsion (Radiation Worker)	41 X-ray Radiography and Accelerator
11 Nuclear Propulsion (Non Radiation Worker)	Radiography < 10 MeV
12 Nuclear Propulsion (Visitor)	42 Accelerator Radiograph => 10 MeV
20 Weapons (Radiation Worker)	43 RADIAC Calibration
21 Weapons (Non Radiation Worker)	44 General Industrial
22 Weapons (Visitor)	50 Research
30 Medical (Diagnostics)	51 Research (Isotopes)
	90 Other

10. Through 14. Leave Blank.
15. Use as appropriate by submitting activity.
16. Printed name and title, and signature, of person submitting report.
17. through 19. Leave Blank.

Copies of this form and other associated radiation dosimetry materials are available on request from the Naval Dosimetry Center. Phone numbers: DSN 295-0142/ 0403/ 6164, Commercial (301) 295-0142/ 0403/ 6164.

APPENDIX B

ANNUAL LIMIT ON INTAKE

The annual limit on intake (ALI) and derived air concentrations (DAC) of some common isotopes as listed in Appendix B, Title 10 Part 20 are provided below.

Isotope	ALI (microcuries) Ingestion	ALI (microcuries) Inhalation	DAC uCi/ml
Americium-241	0.8	0.006	3×10^{-12}
Carbon-14	2,000	2,000	1×10^{-6}
Cesium-137	100	200	6×10^{-8}
Chromium-51	40,000	20,000	8×10^{-6}
Cobalt-60	200	30	1×10^{-8}
Iodine-123	3,000	6,000	3×10^{-6}
Iodine-125	40	60	3×10^{-8}
Iodine-131	30	50	2×10^{-8}
Iridium-192	900	200	9×10^{-8}
Phosphorus-32	600	900	4×10^{-7}
Plutonium-239	0.8	0.006	3×10^{-12}
Radium-226	2	0.6	3×10^{-10}
Strontium-90	30	4	2×10^{-9}
Technetium-99m	80,000	200,000	6×10^{-5}
Thallium-201	20,000	20,000	9×10^{-6}
Thorium-232	0.7	0.001	5×10^{-13}
Tritium (H-3)	80,000	80,000	2×10^{-5}

* ALI and DAC values listed assume the most conservative class. If the chemical form is known, a more appropriate class may be used.